Newlands ess

Chris Phillips

An account of the activities that happened in Newlands Road, Tunbridge Wells, Kent, England, in the period 1947 to 1967. Nearly all about the Children who lived there at the time.

One of the reasons why I have written this book is to help give some encouragement for today's youngsters to start their own stamp club, or any other kind of clubs.

First Published in 2016
By Philcovers (Chris Phillips)

ISBN 978-0-9574259-1-0

Whilst the vast majority of this book is the work of Chris Phillips, some maps scanned from the internet are the copyright of Google. These maps have been accredited. I have also used scans of some photos taken by the Kent & Sussex Courier at the time. Also scans of many press reports in the said paper and many philatelic magazines. Some details of history & geography of the town have also been acquired (from the Town Museum) and reproduced here, which hopefully do not infringe upon anyone's copyright. If any holders of such copyright exist, please accept my apologies, and if you do not wish me to advertise them in any future printings please contact me.

Printed by McRay Press Unit 3 64 - 66 Londesborough Rd, Scarborough, North Yorks, YO12 5AF. 01723 370967
www.mcraypress.co.uk email mike@mcraypress.co.uk
Using Lucida Sans typeface

CONTENTS

Photographs Index

Maps & Photographs

Maps etc

THANKS:-

To Dilys Cluer who spent hours proof reading; without her efforts much grammar and punctuation would not be perfect. To Jonathan Wood the official proof reader. The Tunbridge Wells Library & Museum for their help in allowing me to check the historic records. To all those who have been in contact and reminded me of stuff, people who were THE CHILDREN OF NEWLANDS ROAD at the time: (Using their born names) Peter Powell, John Burton, Bobby Ely, Susanne Ely, Wendy Wells, Colin Fowle, Virginia Timmis, Simon Timmis, Jan Langridge, Sue Laurie, John Teasdale, Chris Yardley, Robert Romer,

Without their help this would not be properly finished.

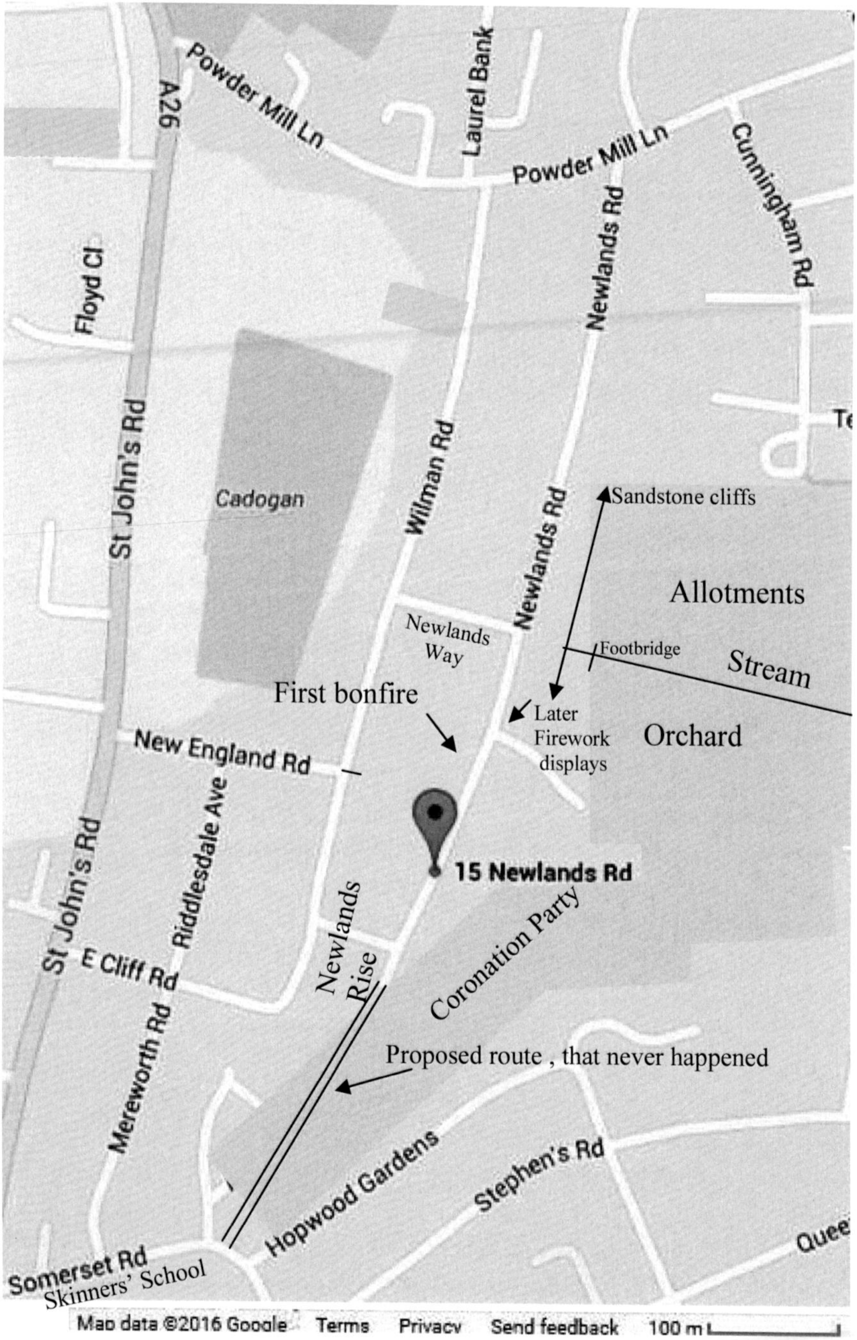
Powder Mill Ln
A26
Laurel Bank
Powder Mill Ln
Cunningham Rd
Newlands Rd
Floyd Cl
St John's Rd
Cadogan
Wilman Rd
Newlands Rd
Sandstone cliffs
Allotments
Newlands Way
Footbridge
Stream
First bonfire
Later Firework displays
Orchard
New England Rd
Riddlesdale Ave
15 Newlands Rd
St John's Rd
E Cliff Rd
Newlands Rise
Coronation Party
Mereworth Rd
Proposed route , that never happened
Hopwood Gardens
Stephen's Rd
Somerset Rd
Skinners' School
Map data ©2016 Google
Terms
Privacy
Send feedback
100 m

1) Newlands Road Beginnings

In the beginning was the land, and the land was alive with trees and plants, and on these plants lived the animals of all kinds; the balance of nature lay undisturbed for many a year. Animals came and went, some never to return. At the same time, cold and heat alternated with wet and dry periods as the land drifted northwards on the upper crust of Planet Earth. Comets and asteroids struck now and again, causing huge disruptions. The land rose and fell as land masses collided; hills became mountains only to be washed back again to flat lands by weathering of rain, floods and wind. The last of the ice melted and the animals who walked upright on two legs began to colonise this land.

Many races moved others on, till the final conquerors displaced the Celts and the Doomsday arrived. Many woodlands became farmlands and the fertile land developed over the millennia began to grow food, nurtured by dedicated two legged mammals. Wells of red running waters were "discovered" nearby, and became a favourite royal watering spa. As a town near Tunbridge grew up around the wells, and expanded, woodlands were felled and a certain area became NEWLANDS FARM. This farm eventually came into the ownership of one William Cheeseman.

The expansion of the town demanded more living space and in the early 1930s the Cheesemans discovered the advantages of selling farm lands for building. A network of roads parallel to the main Tonbridge to the Wells road were laid out. One road was especially wide, as though it were to be a major road to bypass other villages, passing close to the Newlands Farm house, which now owned only a small pocket of low lying fields. Hence this road was called Newlands Road. The short but rather steep road rising at one end was named Newlands Rise, and a middle way through was aptly called Newlands Way, which also led to the driveway down to the remaining farm fields. The road from the St Johns main road was called East Cliff Road, leading at least in part to the cliffs along the east of the south part of Newlands Road. Halfway along, the name changed and it was named after **Wil**liam

Cheese**man** as Wilman Road, and at the top end Wilman and Newlands Road met Powdermill Lane, where there had been plans at one time to continue Newlands Road to take the traffic flows away from the villages on the way to Tonbridge. Gradually, the houses were built on all these roads during the 1930s.

When my parents bought house number 15, the pavements were not yet made up, and planks were in place to walk along the area to be paved; gradually most of the land plot was built up and people took up residence. A few plots in between homes were left to grow wild. Gradually, the pavements were laid with brick, and grass verges left between the pavements and the road. In those days few motor vehicles rolled over the tarred and gravelled surface.

In May 2016, the Tunbridge Wells Museum was good enough to help me find out more about our road, by allowing me to see and copy documents in their archives from the Tunbridge Wells Council in the 1930s. We learnt that our "theory" - that it was to have been a bypass to Tonbridge - was indeed correct. We also found out a few other things, that I will relate here, and also we now have an idea as to why it never became that bypass.

The plans were finally approved on 20th March 1934 to build Newlands Road on what was then called the Newlands Estate.(1). We were shown the plans for the road building. The road was to be constructed in two parts. See the next page for part one, where the biggest surprise was seen. In the place where the road and houses were to be built from number 37 to the Newlands Rise link road, was a large pond. This of course had to be drained before that section could be completed. As far as I know, no one I knew had ever heard of this. (Picture on top of next page). At that time it looked as if Wilman Road was to be as far as the top of Newlands Rise, the other link road, and that the road from St Johns Road was called Eastcliff Road only as far as the 90 degree bend, and the short section between was called The Gardens. Eventually the Eastcliff Road name extended as far as the junction with New England Road, as it is to this day. The plan above clearly shows

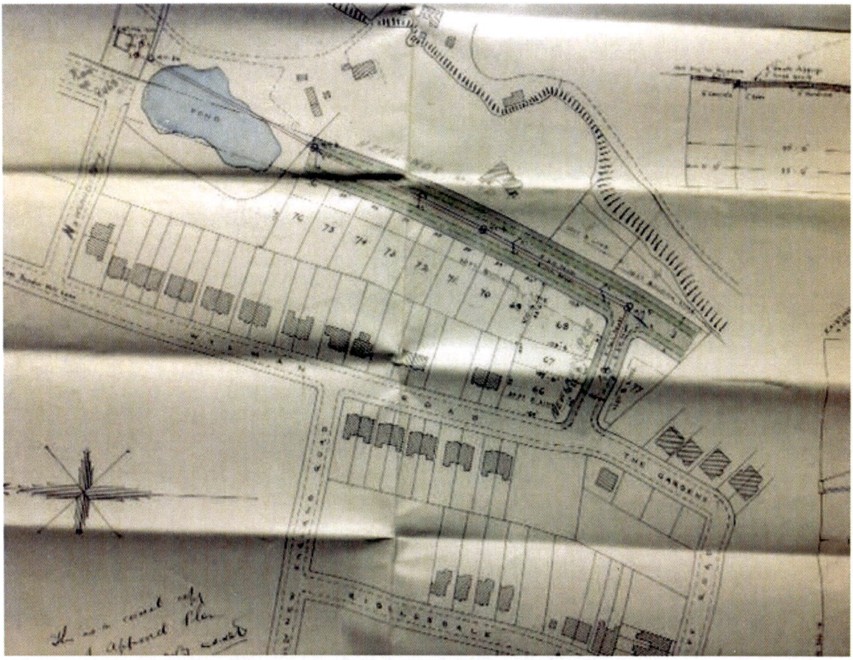

the cliff, from which East Cliff Road got its name.

The next photo, which is in the appendix, shows the plans for the top end of the road from Newlands Way to Powdermill Lane, down which we believed the by-pass was to have been continued, although this never happened.

We also saw an interesting letter from the road builders re the pavements. They were surprised that Newlands Road pavements were to be of BRICK, not tarmac, as were the other pavements. Eventually, the Council had Newlands Road paved with bricks, as was popular in most of Tunbridge Wells.

We also saw documents from people complaining about possibly losing some of their gardens to allow the Newlands Road to join up with Somerset Road, to connect to St John's Road, at the north of The Skinners' School. I believe this must have been one reason why our road never became the Bypass. As a result, to this day all traffic still has to enter Tunbridge Wells via the narrow main streets of Southborough. There is an interesting map in colour in the appendix showing the plans .

I have included in the appendices several more items that we saw relating to the planning.

I also found the plans for our own house (with no 13) and when my father applied for having a garage built in the back garden. When he bought the house he did not want a garage at the side of the house, as several others had; this is shown on the plans too. These plans can also be seen in the appendices.

And then the War came. I entered the world a few weeks before our country decided it had enough of appeasing the German Hitler. Another farmland field was let out to those living near by, as allotments to grow food to help the war effort. In the final year of this terrible conflict, Spitfires were seen chasing invaders overhead, and strange noises were heard high in the sky from the flying bombs on their way to London. Finally the war ended, and after Japan also gave up their disastrous invasions, a victory party was held in a field at the top of the path down to where one entered the allotment areas and to the Cheeseman's bungalow. There was a bonfire and cooking. Now there was a kind of Newlands Road community, and it is this community that will be chronicled in the following chapters.

2) Early Days

MooooOOooo!

My first real memory of my life. I think I must have been about 3 years old. My Mother, I think, showed me to a cow, in a field over a gate or fence. The cow only knowing such a moving language startled my baby brain, and my yelling in fright resulted in my being moved further away from the friendly beast who meant no harm, but had yet to learn the language of the human race; though, apparently in those days cattle were expected to read English, as each gate had a clear black and white notice attached

"CATTLE
PLEASE
SHUT THE GATE".

During the war, though I had no knowledge of there being a war at the time, one of my only three memories was one of hearing a weird, frightening droning "putput" sound in the sky one bright day (in 1944) as I was in the sunny front garden, looking at the bees busy on the flowers. I ran inside, and that was it. The second time was walking home one afternoon with my father on the corner of Eastcliff Road and St Johns Road, and I remember my father pointing up to the sky towards a few Spitfires chasing something high in the clear sky. We then dashed into the porch of the house nearby until they had gone. The third was the "new" Iron (Morrison) Table in our dining room, and one night neighbours came in and we all shared being in this shelter. I remember quite clearly hearing the chanting song being sung all night long:

"This old man, he played one,
He played knick-knack on my thumb;
With a knick-knack paddywhack,
Give the dog a bone,
This old man came rolling home.

This old man, he played two,
He played knick-knack on my shoe;
With a knick-knack paddywhack,
Give the dog a bone,
This old man came rolling home.

This old man, he played three,
He played knick-knack on my knee;
With a knick-knack paddywhack,
Give the dog a bone,
This old man came rolling home.

This old man, he played four,
He played knick-knack on my door;
With a knick-knack paddywhack,
Give the dog a bone,
This old man came rolling home.

This old man, he played five,
He played knick-knack on my hive;
With a knick-knack paddywhack,
Give the dog a bone,
This old man came rolling home.

This old man, he played six,
He played knick-knack on my sticks;
With a knick-knack paddywhack,
Give the dog a bone,
This old man came rolling home.

This old man, he played seven,
He played knick-knack up in heaven;
With a knick-knack paddywhack,
Give the dog a bone,
This old man came rolling home.

This old man, he played eight,
He played knick-knack on my gate;
With a knick-knack paddywhack,
Give the dog a bone,
This old man came rolling home.

This old man, he played nine,
He played knick-knack on my spine;
With a knick-knack paddywhack,
Give the dog a bone,
This old man came rolling home.

This old man, he played ten,
He played knick-knack once again;
With a knick-knack paddywhack,
Give the dog a bone,
This old man came rolling home."

This iron table then later became a work bench and a stage. (See chapter 9).

My first sister, whom I was given the chance to name, Joanna, (I liked at that time a girl at my kindergarten school called Joanna) was born before the end of the war. The only photo I have is one of me on my mother's lap holding Joanna next to our friend Anna, in our back garden. (Photo on next page.)

Anna had come to live with us just before I was born in 1939. She was a schoolgirl aged about 14, from Italy. She was of Jewish parents, and came to live with us because of the persecution of Jews in Italy at the time. Anna later became a Quaker and was a life long friend to our family. As I write, I learned that Anna died recently at the age of 92. I recently attended her memorial in Cambridge Friends Meeting House.

Colin Fowle remembers that one day in 1945 a V2 rocket

landed in the allotments area, but did not explode.

Sometime in 1946 I remember one night Joanna crying all night, and all was silent in the morning. She had died of pneumonia. My first experience of death.

My last kind of experience of the war was really when I was in Kindergarten school, and I remember hearing talk about bombs on Japan and the end of the war finally. And not long after that a street party with a bonfire was held in the last bit of land owned by the Cheesmans, at the top end of the path down to the allotments. There was a big shed, and soup was passed around. It was organised by the Cheesmans. I gathered later in life that was to celebrate the end of the WW2.

Life and living was quite different in those days. Apart from a Hoover and a washing tub, we lived without today's necessities, like fridges, freezers, washing machines, TV, and car. Dad earned money and mum did the housework, though Dad did help with that. Shopping was done most days, and there were regular milk deliveries; I remember Mr King walking with his little electric driven milk cart for years. Before that the cart was pulled by a horse. Most grocers and greengrocers would deliver your orders. I remember often the greengrocer would ring us to see what we wanted that week. Dad had two allotment patches to grow a lot of the seasonal food. We had two apple trees in the back garden and later a pear tree in the front. Most places only had food that was in season - none of these strawberries throughout the year. It was the same with grapes and most fruit. Most fruit and vegetables were English grown. We picked blackberries from the hedgerows, and had jam and jelly-making days in September. Coal and coke was also delivered on a regular basis; we had metal coal bunkers outside our kitchen door. The ashes from the fires were put in the metal dustbins, about a third of the capacity of today's waste bins. The Refuse collector (Dustbin man) would collect your bin once a week and carry it on his shoulders to the dust cart.

Quite a different world.

Now on to what we children did in our street, the main point of this book of real memories.

A Morrison Steel Table, just like the one we had in our dining room, during the air-raids, which later became a work bench in our garage

Chapter 3. 1947 - THE SNOW

Snow is not the only reason why this year is frozen firmly into my brain. I do remember being shown snow out of my bedroom window one earlier winter, and as a result my memories snowballed into any years that I remember snow.

Actually the Snow started in 1946. At the time I did not know why, but later in life it did become clear, as to why this next event took place.

One early December morning in 1946, I knew that we three were going to London to stay with Aunty Winifred, who had a flat there. That morning it started to snow. We had a walk to the bus stop to catch a bus to take us to Tonbridge station to go to London, Charing Cross. What I remember most was not the staying with Aunty (that is very vague), but me seeing the snow covering the footpath, and mum being uncertain about it being slippery. So about 30 minutes before we had to leave, I, using the garden broom, swept a path clear all the 500 yards to the bus stop from our house, along our end of the road and up the steep Newlands Rise, and along East Cliff road to the Bus stop on St Johns Road. By the time we all had to leave to catch the bus, the path was covered in snow again, only it was thinner where my mother walked!

Little did I know at that time that the snow was to stay for 3 whole months. It did disappear temporarily over Christmas, but it returned with renewed vigour afterwards. There were a few false or short periods of thawing. One day I remember new snow falling on partly thawed snow, so that there was an ice layer making a sandwich of snow with a crunchy centre. You could brush off the loose top snow and walk carefully on the iced under surface, which sometimes gave way under my childish wellies!

This is really my first memory of other children and playing on the toboggans, gliding fast down the steep Newlands Rise, (see front cover photo, taken by my father) with someone watching at the bottom in case of the odd car about to try and glide UP the icy road. The drivers, I believe, were not too pleased to see us. We, on the other hand, were not pleased when some cars came steaming up at full speed on tyre chains, which broke up our nice smooth surface.

I remember too having whooping cough for several weeks during this wonderful period of whiteness, taking away much of my enjoyment. I remember too at Kindergarten school looking out of the window and, with the other children ,telling the snow flakes to fall as fast as their legs would carry them!

The other reason why 1947 was an important year for our family was the arrival of my sister Bronwen Miriam. Sadly, I had no say in the choice of her names as I had with Joanna, but I have no quarrel with the choices Mum and Dad made. At that time I had no idea that there was another reason for this year to be important in my life. But that was not to be known till many years later.

The snow finally gave up its life in April that year, followed by a lovely, warm summer, but in some areas the depth of snow did cause much flooding. Bronwen breathed her first breath on August 2nd in the Stonefield Vegetarian Nursing Home in Blackheath, the reason why we had all gone up to London in the previous December. Nearly two months later, at the same nursing home, a certain other young lady made her first appearance in the world, so we almost met my future second wife, Dilys Cluer, and her proud parents.

1948 - 1951 Olympic Games

The Olympic Games have now been to London three times, but 1948 was the first I had heard of them. This was probably the first time that I was expressing my organising ability. For I decided, with the help of the other children in the street, to emulate the international games in our own street. We had several sports, such as 100 yards, long jump, high jump and round the block race (Newlands Road, starting outside our garden, to Newlands Way, Wilman Road, East Cliff Road and down the steep Newlands Rise and back to our gate). I imagine there were a few other sports, but as no records exist I can't be sure. But there was a cycle race, I think. The photo below shows the awards ceremony at the end of all the events in August 1948. My father took the photo from my bedroom, at the

time, unknown to us.

The success of the Newlands Olympics in the London Olympic year was such that we ran them every year for the following 3 years as well, with new races added, including a Slow bicycle race in 1951. By that

Colin Fowle, David Spencer(?); Robert (?) Christine Langridge, Virginia Timmis, Carol Edmonton, Nola Timmis(?) Ian Myers, Peter Wells, Suzanne Ely)

My photo. Robin Grey, Christine Langridge, Carol Edmonton ; Brian Campsie; John Teaadale?; ? ; ? ; ?

time as well, the Kent & Sussex Courier took an interest and posted a photo mock-up of the round the block race start.

The slow bicycle race taken by my father

5) 1950 - 1952 Scout Fairs.

Some of my memories do not always include the reasons why or how we started doing things, and scouting through my brain cells has yet to reveal why I started this three consecutive year annual event in our garden and garage. Perhaps it is lost due to some knots that got tied.

Anyway in 1950 I had a garden fair to raise money for the local scouts, which I later joined when I started at The Skinners' School. Everything was home made: the stalls like Roll a Penny, the throw a soft ball to knock down heavily weighted baked bean tins, pull a string for your prize (cost 6d) as everyone got a prize, you just didn't know what you'd get. I remember very clearly making some Dan Dare Spaceships out of old toilet rolls and corrugated cardboard, and filling them with some sweets or something like that! The Boys Comic (Magazine) "EAGLE" had started that April, and Dan Dare Pilot of the Future was the "star" picture strip story. The first picture shows myself

Bronwen Phillips; myself, Robin Grey, Clive Grey, & Susanne Ely

(nearest the garage door) with Robin & Clive Grey (from next door) and my sister in the doll's cot and her friend, Susanne Ely. These two pictures show the fair open and the local children who came and took part in

the games. My Father took the photos from the bathroom window.

What I failed to mention was that the first day it

rained and at first most of the activities took place in the garage instead of the garden. Each of the fairs (3

Left to right - Robert(?) Colin Fowle, David Spencer, Me, (Not sure), Ian Myers , Bronwen & Keith Spencer. (Kent & Sussex Courier Photo)

I and Ian Myers counting the takings

in all) raised some money for the scouts. I remember one gift we bought was a axe for the scouts to use when on camping week-ends.

6) Living Dangerously

I have called this living dangerously, because when you come to think of it afterwards, some of these next few things which we did were dangerous. When you are children, you often do not know how dangerous something is.

These few events will not necessarily be in the order that they happened, and some were more dangerous than others. Anyone reading this really should **NOT** attempt some of these, at least not without supervision, but children nowadays often do not play in the ways we used to.

Sorry I have no photographic evidence of these.

The first one that I am going to mention is far more dangerous than the rest, I think, and really should not be attempted by anyone.

One day, for some reason, John Burton, Bobby Ely and another boy decided to dig some deep holes in one of the allotments, owned by the father of John Burton. Then they decided to make a tunnel joining one hole to the other. The ground was very much on a clay base, so it was pretty solid. Well, the hole was rather small, and I, being much the smallest and the youngest, was the guinea pig and was volunteered to be the one who actually crawled through. So I dropped to the bottom of one deep hole and emerged and climbed out of the other, much to the amusement of the others. SUCCESS! The ground held up with no support because it was a pretty thick clay. I cannot remember the depth nor the length of the tunnel, but I think the depth was about 6 feet and the tunnel about 3 feet long and 2 feet high. *(John's father made them fill it in, because it would be dangerous.)*

Next was quite different. And above ground. As time went by people used the allotments less and less, and the land owner decided to sell some at the top end of the allotments for building, with a road off Powdermill Lane. Some of us, while the builders were away at the weekends, decided to go and investigate. We climbed up the scaffolding and played chase on the high up platforms at the top of the house being built. Luckily, no one was hurt. And no one came to chase us away.

Another game we played was "he" on the sandstone cliffs above the allotments behind the homes on the East side of Newlands Road, behind the Timmis' house and others. The area was well wooded. I remember climbing up the trees to escape, and succeeded as no one else dared to climb as high as I did on the tops of swaying trees. I even went up one tree and down another.

When young, one does do silly things, just because others do it. I am not sure which year it was, but I must have been about 9 or 10 years old. One of the houses opposite was up for sale, and unoccupied, and one day the older boys whom I was with found the back window of the kitchen was open. The older ones were too large to get in, but they somehow persuaded me to enter via that window and unlock the back door from the inside. I succeeded, and the other three older boys all came in. I took off my wellingtons and left them in the kitchen and we then searched the house, then we heard the police come in and the bigger lads were seen, but being small I was not seen in the wardrobe cupboard that we had all hidden in. They all went down stairs and I stayed. Later I ventured out and crept downstairs and heard the police asking whose wellingtons they were. That was when I owned up. As far as I know no proceedings were taken against anyone, we were just given a warning; we had not done any damage.

Like most youngsters, we were not always aware

of the real dangers. I remember once we fixed a ramp on the pavement outside our house and we cycled as fast as we could and took off. This was not so bad as when, having seen circus tricksters leap on their bikes through a ring of fire, we tried doing something similar but with just a sheet of newspaper. I was the first to take the leap through a sheet of burning newspaper. I came off unscathed, but I had timed it right for when the flames had just parted the sheet, so it just looked like I had cycled through flames. Sadly another younger lad, Simon Timmis, got one piece of burning paper stuck to his skin, and had a nasty burn. We never tried that again.

One more thing, that again must **not** be repeated, is that we learnt how to make our own fireworks. I was taught that we must be gentle when mixing the gunpowder, and not force it into the tubes. Because of this, I never had a dangerous mishap, but I know an older friend (John Burton) did nearly lose one finger making his fireworks, because it blew up in his hand when he was filling it. We did other dangerous things with fireworks. One was to put an empty tin can over a banger. The result was usually two pieces of metal flying through the air, one a circle and the other a rectangle. Anyway, the tin was wrecked, or landed on the neighbour's roof! We also tied a banger on to a rocket stick, with the touch paper facing the rocket jet. We lit the rocket and up it went, but not vertically, but horizontally after the initial rise, and landed near someone's dustbin, and blew the lid off. We hid!

Colin Fowle also remembers firing an air pistol from the other side of the road which hit me between my eyes, leaving a red spot for a few days. He was scared, and never pointed any gun at people again.

7) Street and other Games

Most of the things we did were GOOD things.

In those days cars were a rarity, so the road, the pavements and the grass verges were our usual playground. Obviously there was a lookout for the odd car.

The games we played were things like football, cricket, and a game where we had to throw a ball at any one standing in a circle. You had to name the person, and you had to throw it so that it was POSSIBLE to be caught; if they didn't catch it they lost a life. Once you had lost three lives you had to then go through the mill. This was when all the others lined up along a wall, and leaning with one hand on the wall, you then had to run as fast has you could through the tunnel and try and miss each hand that tried to smack your bottom...

With cricket, there was one garden on the other side of the road, in which the owner was not happy with balls going into their garden. So if the batsman hit the ball into that garden the rule was that you scored 6 runs, you were out, and you had to go and fetch the ball, hoping you'd not be caught!

In winter the games became Snowy games, like snowball

fights, sledging down the steep hill (the car drivers did not like this!) and building GIANT snowmen. One year we built a Family: Mother, Father and Son, on the grass verge.

We also played Cowboys and Indians, with cap pistols, and I introduced the rule: NO ONE SHOOTS TO KILL. Only wounding was allowed! At least that made the games last longer.

One family (Timmis) had bought the plot of land behind their back garden which was small, natural woodland ending on sandstone rocks, overlooking the allotments This was a wonderful place for children to play in. We made tents out of foliage, and climbed trees. We played the usual games like Hide and Seek and "he". Once when playing "he" I climbed up a tree, and being smaller than most for my age, I found I could climb up higher than the others so they could not touch me. I remember swaying about at the top of a tree once, JUST out of reach, and came down the next nearest tree!

Many of the traditional games were also played in the street, such as hopscotch and skipping.

Some people did buy games like Monopoly. Having played it once or twice at a friend's, I decided to make my own version. I think at that time only 3 or 4 versions existed, including London, New York and Paris. So I was the first to have a Tunbridge Wells version. All the streets were changed to Tunbridge Wells street names, and the stations became Central, West, High

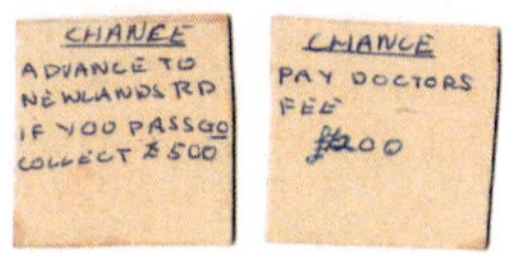

Brooms and Goods Station. Of course Newlands Road was in it, as were all the nearby surrounding streets. The basic rules stayed the same but values were increased to be more in line with prices at the time. I still have the money and the board and all the cards. We used Brick-player bricks for the houses (smallest bricks) and hotels (normal size bricks).

Other games were also played. I remember once playing a game we called school. I have no idea whose idea it was, but about 6 or 7 of us played, 2 boys and the rest girls. The eldest girl (Susanne Ely) was "appointed" (or she wanted to be) the teacher. So the rest were her pupils in class. As teacher she was very "strict". Anyone playing the fool, or who could not answer her questions correctly, was called out to bend over her lap to be spanked by her hand. After the first time that happened to me, I rather liked it and so I made sure I got my answers wrong… I think we played this game only the once or twice.

Another game I remember playing, I think the girls suggested it, was a "kiss chase". The girls would chase the boys and kiss them if they caught them. I remember rather liking one girl (Bronwyn Lloyd Roberts) and kind of let her catch me, and it was rather nice being kissed by her!

In the later years Hula Hoops came into fashion, and I know my sister and her namesake Bronwyn Lloyd-Roberts (in the glasses) had one. The other girl was Sue Norrie. *(This photo is from about 1959 when the hula hooping craze was in full swing - maybe I should say full spin. They were spinning on the pavement outside No. 45 with Nos. 47 and 49 in the background.)*

I expect many children tried this: using two old baked bean cans, two matchsticks and a length of string, one could have a play phone conversation. The string had to be taut, and one used the tin for the speaker and the ear piece. And it worked. Simple technology and cheap. I had one set up from the garden gate to my bedroom.

Recently John Teasdale got in touch with me and reminded me of another game we played in the hot summers. We had a high fence between our back and front gardens, and we had water pistols, and had water fights. We had little "secret" holes bored in the fence, which at first took some by surprise, and we used to climb up the fence, and spray the others with water. I think once we climbed up and threw water from a bucket. Often people would go home rather wet! But I think everyone enjoyed it. Not sure about one or two parents though!

Colin Fowle reminded me that once in a snowy winter an elderly man slipped and fell outside our house, and we somehow got him on a toboggan and took him home. Sadly he had broken his hip, and died a few weeks later.

8) 1951 - 1958 Firework Displays

In the UK, Bonfire Night is on November 5th. On this night it is the tradition to have bonfires in gardens, and to burn a "guy," a dummy dressed in old clothes. This recalls the days in the early 1600s when Guy Fawkes tried to blow up the house of Parliament. He failed and was caught. I'm not sure how true it was that he was burnt on a bonfire, but in those days people were cruel and people were burnt at the stake.

It is on this day that people in the UK also have fireworks. In my youth, most people would have small bonfires and let off a few small fireworks in their back gardens and munch ginger cake and toffee apples around the fire.

Three of the other boys (John Burton, Bobby Ely, and Humphrey Smeeton) in 1951 started the annual street bonfires and firework displays. During the month of October they would call on every house to collect money for fireworks for a STREET celebration, in a plot of land as yet un-built upon. This happened for seven successful years. I helped with these for the fourth such event, and I ran the last three. We introduced a Guy-making com-

Clive Jenkins; ? : ?; John Teesdale; ? ; Bronwen Phillips; Simon Timmis

petition, and a torch light procession. In the later years we asked the Mayor of Tunbridge Wells to be the Judge. (Well, he did happen to live in our road.) The winning Guy was the one carried on a raft in the middle of the procession, The torches were homemade with old wooden poles with firelighters nailed on and lit! When the procession arrived at the bonfire, the guy was fixed to the top of the huge bonfire, and the torches were put on the fire to light it. In the bottom was a special area that had been kept dry, and dry old newspaper put in it to make sure the fire lit. Once it was lit, we let off the fireworks on homemade stands. Thanks to John Burton's father, we managed to get a 10% discount to buy the fireworks (he was the manager of Curry's in Calverley Road) and bought small set pieces. We also made our own fuses to allow us to set off several fireworks together to make a display. On the last three occasions the Mayor of the town (Mr Muffett and Mr Croucher) came to officially open the display. We had big crowds every year, and in the last two we raised money for the Mayor's charity.

Children of Newlands Road, Tunbridge Wells, had their own firework display on Monday and the Mayor (Cr. S. H. Muffett) was there to launch it. The display is now an annual affair and a house-to-house collection is conducted by parents and older children to raise cash to buy the fireworks. This year the organisers are to give a percentage of the money to the Mayor's fund for poliomyelitis.

One year it was so foggy that we had to postpone the event a for few days. Normally we held the event on the right day!

After the first two, the land was built on, and we transferred to the land opposite (owned by the Cheesemans) but that too got built on, and for the last couple of years we could have only the fireworks, as there was no room for a big bonfire as well.

I never knew who was responsible for this little note left (below) in our letter box one year. The point is one of the original organisers (Humphrey) lived in East Cliff Road. So it was natural to include the nearby roads.

Mayor Sent Up The First Rocket

THE fact that big bonfire societies are disbanding on all sides did not worry a happy group of youngsters in Newlands Road on Saturday.

On a small patch of land there they put on their own firework display, as they have done for the last ten years. Money for the show was raised by collection. In previous years there has been a bonfire, but this year, "out of consideration for the neighbours," there was only the display.

There to send the first rocket whizzing into the air was the Mayor of Tunbridge Wells (Cr. S. H. Muffett).

For about an hour a crowd of 200 watched the whirling Catherine wheels, showers of silver stars and coloured fountains, and flinched at the crack of "bangers." Fireworks included a 10s. "Peacock's feather" presented by the Mayor.

The display was organised by Robert Ely, John Burton and Christopher Phillips. They and their helpers collected £13—a record amount.

Mayor of Tunbridge Wells (Cr. S. H. Muffett) lights the first rocket at the Newlands Road firework display

Dear Christopher,
We are sorry for this interruption, but, we would like to inform you, that you are making a mess of the club by inviting outsiders.

ABOUT THE BONFIRE AND FIREWORK DISPLAY.

It is the same about the FIREWORK DISPLAY.
That is to say collecting money from these roads:-
ST. JOHN'S
EASTCLIFT
WILMAN
& POWDERMILL LANE

SIGNED THE DEVIL'S

P.S. WATCH YOUR STEP.

HOUSE TO HOUSE COLLECTIONS ACT
Collector's Certificate of Authority

Block Letters C. J. PHILLIPS

of 15. NEWLANDS Road
TUNBRIDGE WELLS

is hereby authorised to collect for The Newlands Road Firework Display on behalf of Doctor Barnados Homes

in The Newlands Road Area

during the period 9th Oct. – 5th Nov 1957.

Signed:— C. J. Phillips.
(Chief Promotor)

Signature of Collector
C. J. Phillips

We got official permission to do the collection. Each Collector had to have this certificate with them.

6th

NEWLANDS ROAD FIREWORK DISPLAY
AT
Mr. Cheeseman's Field
ON
MONDAY NOVEMBER THE FIFTH AT
6.30.pm.
OPENED BY:-
HIS WORSHIP THE MAYOR OF TUNBRIDGE
WELLS, Mr. MUFFET.
TOURCHLIGHT PROCESSION (6.15.pm)
Starts at the TOP of Newlands Road
(For the Children Only)
Please Come You WILL enjoy it.
NO Bonfire this year.
There will be a collection during
the Display for the Mayor's
Fund for POLIO.

THE SEVENTH ANNUAL
NEWLANDS RD. FIREWORK
DISPLAY
ON
TUESDAY NOVEMBER THE FIFTH, AT
6.30.pm.
In Mr CHEESMANS FIELD, To be
OPENED BY,
HIS WORSHIP THE MAYOR OF ROYAL TUNBRIDGE
WELLS.
(Councillor E. Croucher J.P.)
TORCHLIGHT PROCESSION (for the children)
6.15.pm.
(starts at Top of Newlands Road)
ROFITS WILL GO TO THE DOCTOR
BARNARDO'S HOMES.
RE WILL BE A COLLECTION DURING
E DISPLAY. (for Vistiors who have
NOT ALREADY CONTRIBUTED)
YOU AND YOUR FRIENDS ARE
INVITED TO COME, YOU WILL ENJOY IT.
P.T.O.

Two posters
1966 & 1967

HOUSE TO HOUSE
COLLECTIONS ACT

NEWLANDS ROAD
FOREWORK DISPLAY
on behalf of the
DOCTOR BARNADO'S
HOMES.

AUTHORISED
COLLECTOR'S BADGE

Letter of permission
and the badge we had
to wear when collecting
door to door

KENT COUNTY CONSTABULARY

Tel.: 3205

All official communications to be addressed to "The Superintendent of Police."

POLICE STATION.
Tunbridge Wells.

Our Ref.: E.7086/57

Your Ref.:

24th October, 1957

Dear Sir,

In reply to your letter of the 23rd instant, I have to inform you that there will be no objection to your proposed 'Torchlight Procession' on the 5th November, next, provided that no obstruction or annoyance is caused.

Yours faithfully,

Superintendent.

Mr.C.Phillips,
15 Newlands Road,
Tunbridge Wells,
Kent.

THE 7th
NEWLANDS ROAD
IREWORK DISPLAY.
TUESDAY NOV. 5th.
In Mr. Cheesemans Field at 6-30pm.
OPENED BY:-
IS WORSHIP THE MAYOR OF
TUNBRIDGE WELLS.
ORCHLIGHT PROCESSION
6=15 p.m.

THE NEWLANDS ROAD FIREWORK DISPLAY 1954

Starts at 6 p,m, (app,) in Mr, Cheesamans field Newlands Road, at 5, 45,p,m, two gallons of paraffin will be poured onto the BONFIRE , at 6 p,m, 8 3d rockets will be set off and the show will begin: At 7p,m, the TORCHLIGHT PROCESSION will comence at the end of NEWLANDS ROAD, there wil be about 20 'Torches' The First I5 children to aply for a 'Torch', under I6 and over 9 will get one free of charge, The procession will move down NEWLANDS ROAD to the field the guy will be placed on and the torches will be thrown on, and the bonfire will be lit:

There will be a prize for the best guy of 2/6 box of FIREWORKS, also a 6d rocket, the wining GUY will go with the TORVHLIGHT PROCESSION, (ANY speling mistakes here the person who finds the most by NOVEMBER THE Ist, receives afirework)

Put your names hrer for the TORCHLIGHT PROCESSION?

AGE	NAME	ADDRESS	NO.
10	Ralcon Cliff.	51 Newlands Road	1
13½	Colin Fowle.	5. Newlands Rd.	2
12¾	Virginia Timms	40. Newlands. Rd.	3
12.	M. Ashby.		4
			5
			6
			7
			8
			9
			10
			11
			12
			13
			14
			15

ALL CHILDREN ~~UNDER~~ THE AGE OF IO -8 WILL RECEIVE A'BROKS 2 BANGER IF THEY SEE ME BEFORE NOV 1st, UNDER 8'S WILL RECEIVE A HAND HOLDER ON NOV: 5th, If they live in N.R. N. Rise., N. Way, Eastcliff and Willman Road.

LAST YEAR WE COLLECTED ABOUT £19, and GAVE £4 TOWARDS THE MAYOR'S POLIO FUND,(out of this), WE WOULD LIKE TO TAKE THIS OPPORTUNITY TO THANK ALL THOSE WHO CONTRIBUTED LAST YEAR, & ASK YOU TO HELP AGAIN THIS YEAR. THERE WILL BE THE USUAL HOUSE TO HOUSE COLLECTION, AND THE COLLECTION DURING THE DISPLAY.

IF YOU HAVE ANY CHILDREN WHO WANT TO TAKE PART IN THE TORCHLIGHT PROCESSION PLEASE TELL THE OFFICIAL COLLECTOR WHEN HE COMES ROUND.

MAP

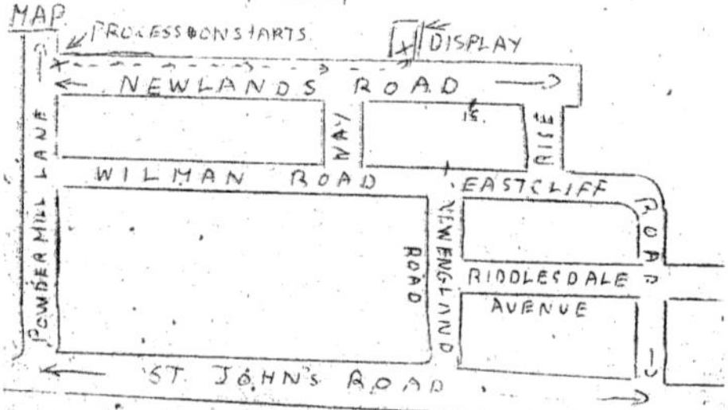

ORGANIZERS: — C. J. Phillips (15 Newlands) and J. Burton.

PLEASE KEEP ALL PETS INDOORS ON THE 5th OF NOVEMBER.

MAYOR'S PARLOUR,
TUNBRIDGE WELLS.

COUNCILLOR ERNEST CROUCHER, J.P.
MAYOR

8th October, 1957.

Dear Sir,

His Worship the Mayor has asked me to thank you for your kind invitation to the Annual Fire Work Display at 6.30 p.m. on November 5th, and to say that it will give him great pleasure to attend.

Yours faithfully,

Mayor's Secretary.

C. Phillips, Esq.,
15, Newlands Road,

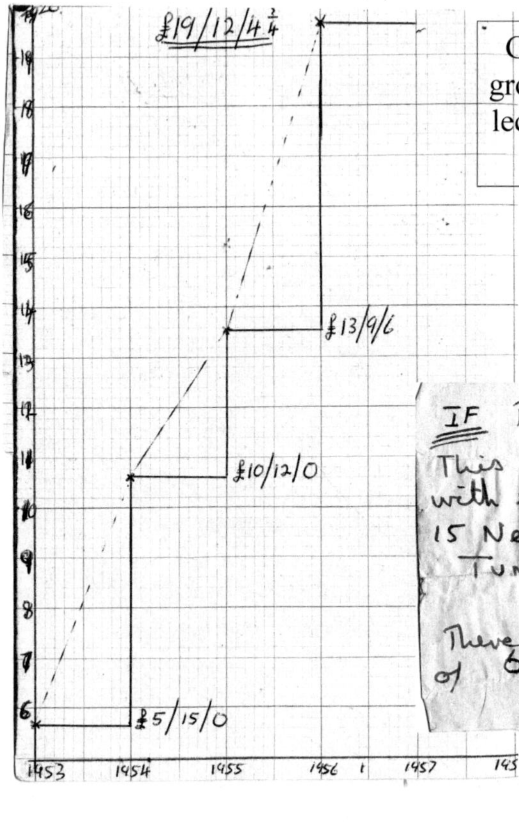

Graph showing the growth in money collected over the past 4 years

We gave a prize to finders of any of our rocket sticks returned.

IF The Finder returns
This rocket stick complete
with empty case to
15 Newlands Road
TUNBRIDGE WELLS
Kent
There will be a prize
of 6^d for him.

THE 5th NEWLANDS ROAD FIREWORK DISPLAY OF 1955 For Stand 3

C. Phillips

	Dis: NO:	Stand No:	No of f'works	Total cost	Make	Description
	1	1	1	5/-	Standard	Rocket
	2	4	4	6/-	Brocks	Spangle Shells
Rob	3	3	3	6/-	"	Cascades
	4	4	3	6/-	Standard	Roman candle set pieces
	5	1	3	6/-		Rockets
	6	2	1	3/-	Standard	Chinese Flyer
	7	4	2	3/-	Brocks	Jack in the boxes
Me	8	3	2	4/-	Brocks	Cascades
	9	4	4	8/-	Brocks	Silver rains
Rob	10	3	2	4/-	Standard	Jack in the boxes
	11	1	3	9/-		Rockets
Me	12	3	1	5/-	Standard	Roman Candle set piece
	13	4	1	3/-	Brocks	Mine of serpents
	14	2	2	4/-	Standard	Motor Wheels
Rob	15	3	3	6/-	Standard	Screechers at 2/- each
	16	4	2	4/-	Standard	Cascades
Me	17	3	1	5/-	Standard	Roman Candle set piece
	18	1	3	6/-		Rockets
	19	4	2	3/-	Brocks	Guy Fawkes Mines
Robin	20	3	2	6/-	Brocks	Roman Candles
	21	2	1	3/-	Standard	Chinese Flyer
Me 22	22 (23)	4 (3)	2 (1)	4/- (10/-)	Standard	Cascades PEACOCKS FEATHER
Rob	23 (24)	3	1	5/-	Standard	Devil among the Tailors
	24 (25)	1	3	9/-		Rockets
Me	25 (26)	3	3	4/6	Pains	Coloured Lights
	26 (27)	2	1	5/-	Standard	Vertical Wheel
Rob	27 (28)	3	1	3/-	Brocks	Jack in the box
	28 (29)	4	1	5/-	Brocks	Roman Candle set piece
Me 30	29 (30)	3	4	6/-	Brocks	Bomb Shells
	30 (31)	4	2	4/-	Standard	Jack in the boxes
	31 (32)	1	3	6/-		Rockets
	32 (33)	4	2	4/-	Standard	Cascades
Rob	33 (34)	3	4	6/-	Brocks	Roman Candles
	34 (35)	2	2	4/-	Standard	Motor Wheels
	35 (36)	4	2	3/-	Mine of serpents	Brocks
Me	36 (37)	3	4	4/-	Brocks	Star Shells
38	37	1 (4)	3 (2)	6/- (4/-)	STANDARD	Rockets MINE OF SERENTS
41	38	4	3	6/-	Standard	Roman Candle set pieces
Rob 40	39	3	1	3/-	Brocks	Jack in the box
	40 (42)	4	4	6/-	Standard	Screechers
	41 (43)	2	1	5/-	Standard	Vertical Wheel
	42 (44)	4	2	6/-	Brocks	Roman Candles
Me	43 (45)	3	1	5/-	Standard	Devil among Tailors
	44 (46)	1	3	9/-		Rockets
	45 (47)	2	3	12/-	S,B,S	1 Cascade, 2 5/- Wheels (Set piece)

At 6-15 there will be a Torch light Procession

Total cost this year is £13 ; 2 : 6

The programme of fireworks; there were four young people in charge of the four stands

THE 6th Newlands Road Firework Display (Stand No. 1, 15 items).

Item No	Stand No	No of F'ws	The Fireworks	Make
1	R	1 @ 5/-	The Mayors Rocket	S
2	W	1 @ 5/-	Vertical Wheel	S
3	1	2 @ 3/-	Roman Candle Set Pieces	S
4	2	1 @ 5/-	Battery of Screechers -	S
5	R	3 @ 3/-	Rocets	S
6	W	2 @ 2/-	Motor Wheels	S
7	1	3 @ 1/6	Bomb Shells	B
8	2	3 @ 2/-	Cascades	S
9	R	3 @ 2/-	Rockets	S
10	W	2 @ 3/-	Chinese Flyers	S
11	1	3 @ 2/-	Roman Candle Set Pieces	S
12	2	2 @ 3/-	Devil among the Taiors	S
13	R	3 @ 3/-	Rockets	B
14	W	1 @ 3/-	Vertical Wheel	S
15	1	3 @ 1/6	Bomb Shells	B
16	2	3 @ 2/-	Jack in the Boxes	S
17	1	3 @ 2/-	Silver Rains	B
18	2	2 @ 2/-	Air Bombs	S
19	R	3 @ 2/-	Rockets	S
20	W	2 @ 2/-	Motor Wheels	S
21	1	3 @ 2/-	Screechers	S
22	2	1 @ 3/-	Parachute	S
23	1	2 @ 3/-	Roman Candle Set Pieces	S
24	2	3 @ 1/6	Coloured Fires	P
25	I	1 @ 10/-	Peacock's Feather	S
26	2	3 @ 2/-	Mine of Serpents	S
27	R	1@ 5/-	Rocket	B
28	W	1 @ 5/-	Vertical Wheel	S
29	1	2 @ 3/-	Roman Candles	S
30	2	3 @ 2/-	Cascades	B
31	1	3 @ 2/-	Screechers	S
32	2	3 @ 2/-	Jack in the Boxes	S
33	R	3 @ 3/-	Rocets	S
34	W	2 @ 2/-	Motor Wheels	S
35	1	3 @ 1/6	Bomb Shells	B
36	2	2 @ 3/-	Devils among the Tialors	S
37	1	2 @ 1/6, 1 @ 3/-.	Roman Candles Set Pieces	PS
38	R	3 @ 2/-	Rockets	S
39	W	2 @ 3/-	Chinese Flyers	S
40	1	3 @ 2/-	Roman Candle Set Pieces	S
41	2	2 @ 1/6, 1 @ 2/-	2 Coloured Fires, 1 Mt. Everest	P
42	1	3 @ 1/6	Bomb Shells	B
43	2	3 @ 2/-	Cascades	B
44	R	3 @ 3/-	Rockets	S
45	W	1 @ 5/-	Vertical Wheel	S
46	2	1 @ 3/-	Parachute	S
47	1	3 @ 2/-	Roman Candle Set Pieces	S
48	2	1 @ 5/-	Battery of Screechers	S
49	R	3 @ 3/-	Rockets	S
50	W	1 @ 10/-	'FOUNTAIN'. (1 Vertical Wheel, one Triangle Wheel, 1 Cascade.)	S SB

The programme of fireworks; there were three young people in charge of the four stands

M.J.H. GIRLING, LL.B.
SOLICITOR

TOWN CLERK JA/EK

TELEPHONE NO. 2822
Extn. 5.

TOWN HALL
TUNBRIDGE WELLS

8th October, 1957,

Dear Sir,

I have to acknowledge receipt of your application for a licence to promote a House to House collection within the Borough. You will appreciate that this is a matter which has to be put before a Committee of the Council before a decision can be given. The next meeting of the Committee will take place on the 24th October next, and I am afraid that I cannot give you any definite information until after that date. In the meantime of course, no collection should be made.

Yours faithfully,

Town Clerk.

C. Phillips, Esq.,
15, Newlands Road,
TUNBRIDGE WELLS.

THE 7th. ANNUAL NEWLANDS ROAD FIREWORK DISPLAY, NOV. 5th. 1957.

6-15 pm. Torchlight Procession starts at top of N.R.
6-30 pm. Display Starts.

Item.	Stand.	Fireworks. etc.
1	R	~~The Mayor~~'s Rocket @5/- (OPENING)
2	2	1 battry af Bombshells @ 7/6
3	W	1 Verticle Wheel @ 5/-
4	1	2 Roman Candle Set Pieces @ 3/-
5	R	3 Rockets @3/- (Brock's)
6	W	2 Motor Wheels @ 2/-
7	1	3 Bomb Shells @ 1/6.
8	2	3 Cascades @ 2/-
9	1	3 Golden Rains @ 2/-
10	2	3 Prismatic Lights @ 1/6.
11	W	1 Turbo Jet @ 7/6
12	1	1 R. C. Set Piece @ 5/- (Brock's)
13	2	3 Mines of Serpents @ 2/-
14	R	3 Rockets @ 2/-.
15	W	1 Chineze Flyer. @ 3/-
16	1	1 R.C. Set Piece @ 5/-
17	2	1 Battery of Screechers @ 5/-
18	1	2 R.C. Set Pieces @ 3/-
19	2	3 Cascades @ 2/-
20	R	3 Rockets @ 2/-
21	W	1 Chineze Flyer @ 3/-
22	1	1 ~~RxC~~. Star @ 10/- (not fused) (Broken)
23	2	1 Battery of Screechers @ 5/6
24	R	3 Rockets @ 3/- (Standard)
25	W	1 'Fountain' (2 Verticle Wheels, @ 5/- & 3/-, and
26	1	1 Latice. @ 10/- (not fused)
27	2	1 Devil among the tailors @ 5/-
28	R	3 Rockets @ 2/-
29	W	2 Motor Wheels @ 2/-
30	1	2 R.C. Set Pieces @ 3/-
31	2	1 Battery of Screechers @ 5/-
32	R	3 Rockets @ 3/- (Brock's)
33	W	1 Chineze Flyer @ 3/-
34	2	3 Prismatic Lights @ 1/6.
35	1	1 R.C. Set Piece @ 5/-
36	2	1 Battery of BombShells @ 7/6
37	W	2 Motor Wheels @ 2/-
38	1	4 Traffic Lights @ 1/- (one upside down)
39	2	1 Devils among the Taylors @ 5/-
40	R	3 Rockets @ 3/- (Standard)
41	W	1 Chinese Flyer @ 3/-
42	1	1 R.C. Set Piece @ 5/-
43	2	1 Battery of Screechers @ 5/6
44	1	1 Star @ 15/- (Not fused)
45	2	3 Jack in the boxes @ 2/-
46	1	2 R.C. Set Pieces @ 3/-
47	2	3 Cascades @ 2/-
48	R	3 Rockets @ 3/- (Standard)
49	W	1 Verticel Wheel @ 5/

all values to omitted in Mayor's copy.

The programme of fireworks; there were four young people in charge of the four stands

9. 1953 Newlands Road Club & other clubs.

The year was 1953, and the whole country was getting excited by the coming coronation in June.

The last such occasion had been in 1937, which had been planned for King Edward 8th, with much publicity and excitement, which was suddenly dashed because unknown to most of the British public (but not to some foreign nations (!)) the Prime Minister and the Archbishop of Canterbury and others had firmly led him to declare his abdication on Dec 10th, to a rather shocked nation, for he had been the "people's" King. The reason given was his undying love for a USA divorcee, Wallis Simpson. But there may have been other, more political, reasons as well. At the time I knew nothing about all that. The result was a sudden change in person to be crowned in May 1937: his brother, who became King George 6th, one who did not want to be king, and had a voice impediment. But during the war, the public took to loving him and his wife for the way they behaved during those war years.

I remember distinctly walking home one Saturday lunch time on 6th Feb 1952. It was a mild day for the time of year and the sun was shining, and as I walked past number 5 Newlands Road, on my way home from school, Colin Fowle, who lived there, and was a few years younger than me, called out "Have you heard?"

"What?" I replied.

"The King died last night".

"OH!" was all I could say.

Princess Elizabeth went up into a tree in Kenya on Feb 5th and descended the next day as Queen. So for the next 15 months the coronation of Queen Elizabeth was planned for June 1953. She and the royal court had not expected George to die whilst she was away on a tour. It was of lung cancer, and in general the public were not informed, except to say he was ill.

It was in April the following year that the great event - though not recorded in officialdom at the time, but only in a new exercise book - that the event that changed my life for the rest of my years, happened.

One early April Saturday lunch time, in 1953, KNOCK

KNOCK KNOCK.

Mum, Dad, Bronwen & myself were just finishing lunch in our dining room. At that time no one had any idea that those knocks were going to lead to a historic club being formed, and that the very room that we were eating in would be the meeting place many a time when important visitors came to give talks and displays to young people in our street.

It was a Saturday. I and Dad had just come home from The Skinner's School. Dad was a Maths teacher there, and I was in the third year, 3A. Yes, we did have school every Saturday morning; this was a throwback to the early days of the school, before it became state run, but governed by the Skinners' Company (London). Originally, it was a private school run by "The Skinners' Company, London". It was one of four schools: one in Tunbridge Wells (all boys), one in London (girls) and two all boys in Tonbridge (The Judd School, and the Public School). The Judd School and The Skinners' School came under the Kent County Council some time after the end of WW2, but kept the Governors as The Skinners' Company. The girls' school came under the London Schools Board. The Tonbridge Public School stayed under total control of the Company, and was fee paying.

Anyway, back to the Knock Knock, and who was there. (Not Dr Who, I might add! But you might wonder WHO!)

Colin Fowle and Robin and Clive Grey were standing there with a little booklet, as I opened the door.

Colin and Clive were younger than me, and Robin was older. The Greys lived next door at No 13, and Colin at number 5. Colin went to St George's School (a private one in Tunbridge Wells), and the brothers Grey went to a boarding Catholic school somewhere near by, near Crowborough, I think.

"As you are so good at organising things, we were wondering if you could start a Stamp club for us," they said, and handed me a copy of "STAMP FINDER", open at the back page.

I was rather taken aback, and had a brief look at the page, and said that I would look at the booklet and see what I could do. I said goodbye, and returned to finish my pudding.

Anyway, I read the article and thought about it.

A few days later, I called a meeting of all children in the street in our garage. In the back end of the garage was the wartime steel table (Morrison Steel Table), under which we had slept a few times (with neighbours) in the dining room, during the end of the war. It was now the work table for Dad to use in the garage. We never used the garage for a car. In fact we never had a car till the mid 1960s anyway.

So with a garage full of children from the street we first elected a committee for the NEWLANDS ROAD CLUB, a club to oversee all other clubs.

I was elected Chief. The minutes showed that David Spencer was elected Secretary.

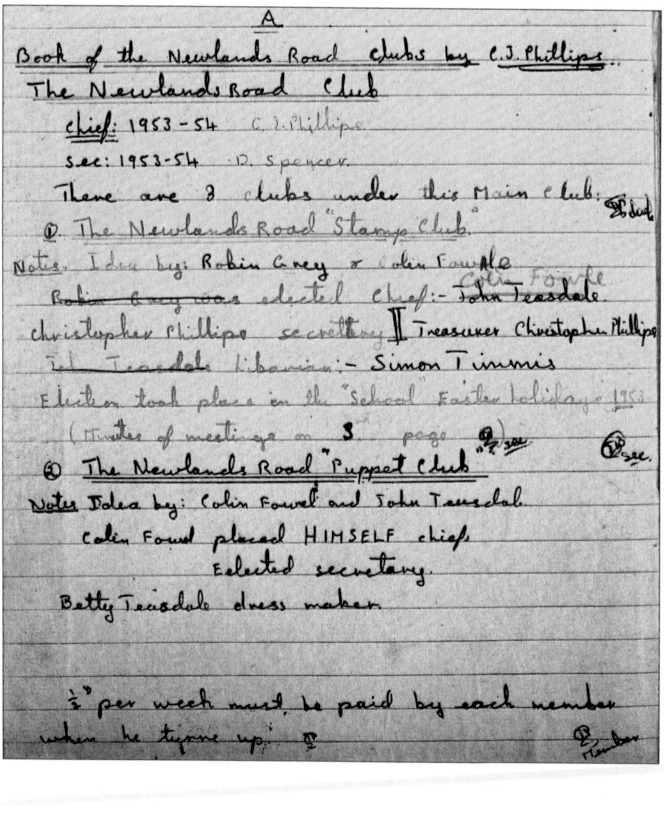
A
Book of the Newlands Road clubs by C.J. Phillips.
The Newlands Road Club
Chief: 1953-54 C. J. Phillips
Sec: 1953-54 D. Spencer
There are 3 clubs under this Main club.
1. The Newlands Road "Stamp Club"
Notes. Idea by: Robin Grey & Colin Fowle
~~Robin Grey was~~ elected chief:- ~~John Teasdale~~ Colin Fowle
Christopher Phillips secretary Treasurer Christopher Phillips
~~John Teasdale~~ Librarian:- Simon Timmis
Election took place in the "School" Easter holidays 1953
(Minutes of meetings on 3rd page)
2. The Newlands Road "Puppet Club"
Notes Idea by: Colin Fowel and John Teasdal.
Colin Fowl placed HIMSELF chief.
Eelected secretary.
Betty Teasdale dress maker.
½d per week must be paid by each member when he turns up.

Then we held elections for the Stamp Club. Robin Grey was elected Chief (it was his idea) and I was elected Secretary. And it seems I became treasurer more or less by default, to handle the money raised at auctions. John Teasdale was

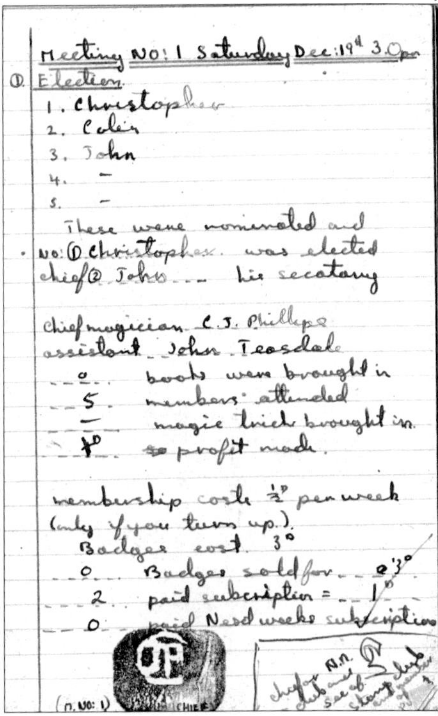

Meeting NO: 1 Saturday Dec 19th 3.0pm
① Election
1. Christopher
2. Colin
3. John
4. –
5. –
These were nominated and
No: ① Christopher was elected
chief ② John ... his secretary

chief magician C.J. Phillips
assistant John Teasdale
0 books were brought in
5 members attended
– magic trick brought in.
0d no profit made.

membership costs ½d per week
(only if you turn up).
Badges cost 3d
0 Badges sold for 0/3d
2 paid subscription = 1d
0 paid Next weeks subscription
(M. NO: 1) CHIEF

elected Librarian.

The rest of the story of the stamp club will follow in its own chapters. As it was such a huge success it deserves its own story.

Two other clubs came under the scrutiny of the Street club. First there was the Puppet club, I think run by Colin Fowle and Virginia Timmis. They had a few meetings making puppets and their clothes, but sadly it closed after a few meetings.

At that time I had several boys' books on how to do magic with cards and other stuff, and how to make some tricks. (Most of these I still have.) I had actually performed a magic trick in public in Bexhill. When we went to Bexhill for our summer holidays, I was interested in the Punch and Judy show and even more so in the puppeteer's Magic show afterwards. In 1952 I asked him if I could do a trick, and he let me. I had a young girl assistant (who happened to be staying at the same guest house) and I did my trick, much to the applause of the pub-

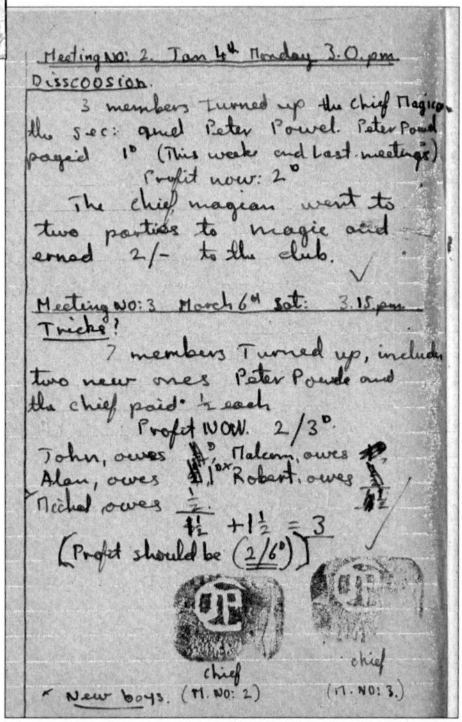

Meeting NO: 2. Jan 4th Monday 3.0.pm
Disscoosion.
3 members Turned up the chief Magician the sec: and Peter Powel. Peter Powel payeid 1d (This week and Last meetings)
Profit now: 2d
The chief magian went to two parties to magic and erned 2/- to the club.

Meeting NO:3 March 6th sat: 3.15pm
Tricks!
7 members Turned up, including two new ones Peter Powde and the chief paid ½ each
Profit NOW. 2/3d.
John, owes ½d Malcom, owes ½
Alan, owes ½ Robert, owes ½
Michael owes ½
1½ + 1½ = 3
(Profit should be (2/6d))
chief chief
New boys. (M. NO: 2) (M. NO: 3.)

lic! I have done magic tricks at several parties since. For those who use YouTube, I have recorded myself doing a few of these bits of "magic"!

So a few months later I started a Magic Circle club, for which I do have a few records, and we did learn a few conjuring tricks, and I did a few magic tricks at parties. But sadly, though I personally never lost my interest in magic, the club also floundered after a few meetings.

There was one other club that I knew about, and that was started by my sister Bronwen and her friend Susanne Ely. They

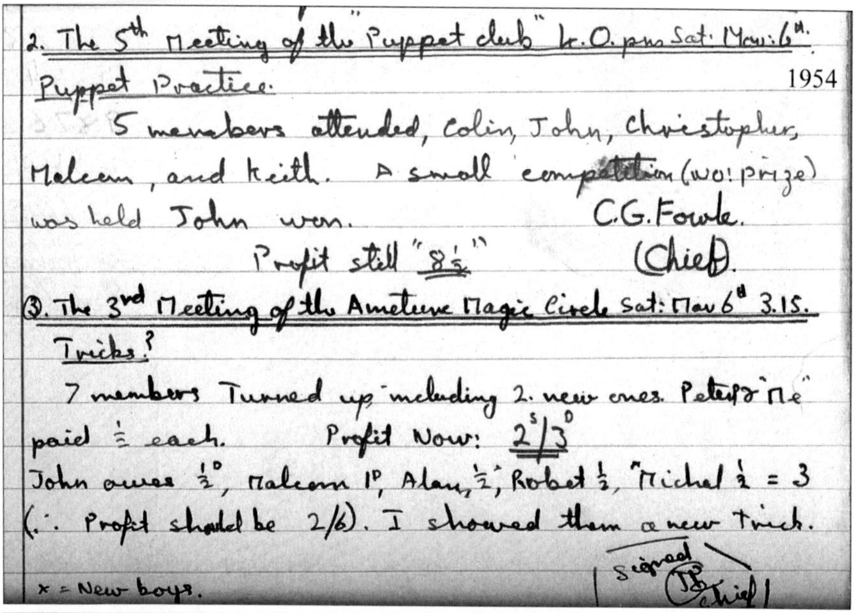

2. The 5th Meeting of the "Puppet club" 4.0. pm Sat: Mar: 6th.
Puppet Practice. 1954
5 members attended, Colin, John, Christopher, Malcom, and Keith. A small competition (NO! prize) was held John won. C.G.Fowle.
Profit still "8½" (Chief).
③. The 3rd Meeting of the Ameteure Magic Circle Sat: Mar 6th 3.15.
Tricks?
7 members Turned up including 2. new ones. Peter & Me paid ½ each. Profit Now: 2/3
John owes ½d, Malcom 1d, Alan ½, Robert ½, Michel ½ = 3
(∴ Profit should be 2/6). I showed them a new trick.
signed JB Chief
x = New boys.

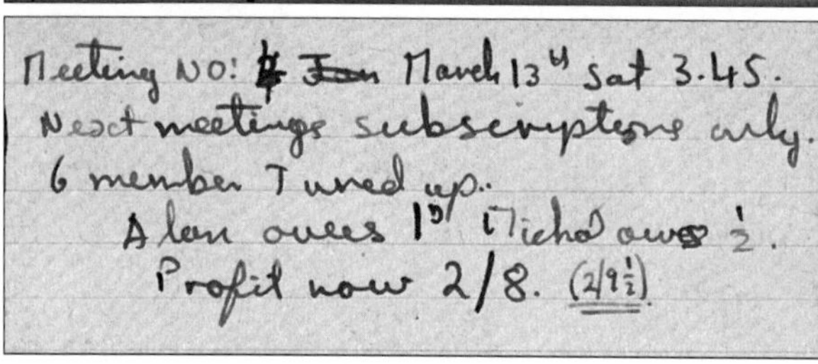

Meeting NO: 4 March 13th Sat 3.45.
Next meetings subscriptions only.
6 member Turned up.
Alan owes 1d Michel owes ½.
Profit now 2/8. (2/9½)

started it because they had been told they were too young to be members of the stamp club. They met once a week on our front doorstep. I remember asking what the club was, and was told that it was a "Milk Bottle Top Collecting and Bible Reading Club".

Every week they looked at their milk bottle tops and read out passages from the Bible.

The only club that remained was the stamp club, and that is another story. I still have the record books of the meetings: see the picture below.

We did not know it, at the time, but this was the start of something big. Something that grew to being known not only around the streets where we lived, but in the town, in the country, in the Post Office, and even Parliament. And it did not finish there, the stamp world got to know, yes around the WORLD!

That story will be told in more detail in later chapters, but it has to be mentioned briefly here as it was also the start of the era of the Newlands Road clubs.

Thanks to the Facebook Group for Newlands Road,
https://www.facebook.com/groups/NewlandsRd/?fref=ts
a few others have come to light. I have no information on these, other than that they existed:

The Newlands Road Nature Club
(Later became the N R Science Club)
The Good Companions
The Tudor Rose Stamp Club
The Kember Friendly Society .

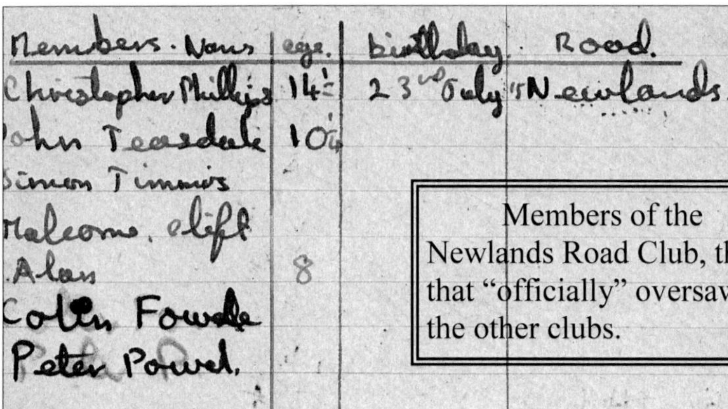

Members. Name	age.	birthday	Road.
Christopher Phillips	14½	23rd July	Newlands
ohn Teasdale	10¼		
imon Timmins			
Malcolm, Cliff			
Alan	8		
Colin Fowle			
Peter Powel,			

Members of the Newlands Road Club, the one that "officially" oversaw all the other clubs.

10) 1953 Coronation Street Party.

18 months after the new Queen had descended from a tree house in Kenya, with much planning and huge publicity, the second Elizabeth was crowned Queen of England. She was the first Queen Elizabeth for Scotland, so some Scottish people were quite upset that she was to be called Queen Elizabeth the second, and there were protests.

In another instance of Scottish protest, the Stone of Scone had been stolen from the coronation chair in Westminster Abbey, but it was found before the coronation.

The Coronation Stone is a large block of red sandstone, with chisel marks on top, thought by some to be the Stone of Destiny. The Stone of Destiny was said to have been used by St Columba, as a travelling altar. For centuries Scottish kings sat upon the Stone to be crowned. The Stone was first stolen from Scone Abbey in 1296 by the English King Edward I. Geologically, it resembles the local Scone sandstone. The Stone was fitted into a wooden seat called St Edward's Chair, and placed in Westminster Abbey, London. During a phase of Scottish nationalism in 1950, four Scots students entered the Abbey early on Christmas Day and stole the Stone from beneath the coronation throne. They dropped it by accident and it broke in two. They loaded the Stone into their car boot. According to *The Times, Dec 1950,* a futile police hunt for the Stone led to a compromise: it was to be left at Arbroath Abbey, site of the famous Declaration of 1320, draped in a Saltire. The Home Secretary decided that it was not in the public interest to prosecute the four Glasgow University students who had stolen the Stone. Anyway, the stone was in place for the Corona-

Our Coronation Bunting

tion of 1953.

Ours was one of many streets to have a Coronation Party. I am not quite sure how this came about, but I know my Dad had a great deal to do with it. As to the number of people involved in our street, as far as I can remember this was actually the biggest single event ever organised for the street. The numbers attending may not have reached the numbers who came to the annual firework displays, but the organisation was certainly much bigger. We were lucky in that the Cheesemans still owned one small field in the valley, and they allowed us to make good use of this. (This field no longer exists as it is built over with a street and houses.)

There are three main things I remember most about this day. One was the Play "The Mad Hatter's Tea Party" that my dad wrote for some of us children to perform at the party. I think I was the Mad Hatter, and Bronwen (my sister) was the dormouse, but she had flu that day and someone else had to be the dormouse. John Teasdale became the Dormouse, but can't remember who Alice was, nor the March Hare. Anyway I think it went well. The second thing was that we had some races, this time on the field and not on the pavement. There was a small marquee for serving refreshments. John remembers winning a prize in a race

And the last thing was the first thing... Our next door neighbours (Hodgsons) had a TV. Most of us did not in those days. They were away for the week, and gave us permission to watch the coronation on their TV; my parents had the key. So many of us (several families) crammed into their living room and were watching the black and white BBC coverage, and then a Policeman called! He was amazed that an empty house was full of people! In those days if you were going to leave your house empty for more than a couple of days, you informed the police and they kept an eye on it. No alarms in those days! And the Police regularly patrolled every street. Anyway that was sorted…

How to Organize a Stamp Club

MORE FUN FOR COLLECTORS

You will find that the hobby of stamp collecting is twice as much fun if you make a practice of talking and swapping stamps with other collectors. The best way to accomplish this is by belonging to a stamp club, for a club enables you to increase your knowledge of stamps, dispose of your duplicates in exchange for stamps you want, and participate in enjoyable club activities all at the same time. If there is not already a stamp club in your neighbourhood, it should be an easy matter to get several of your friends together to form one

Many people, also, are in a favourable position to sponsor enjoyable group activities by introducing philately and starting a stamp club within some larger organization. In public and private schools, summer camps, business firms, churches, libraries, scout troops and Y.M.C.A.'s there is often a real need for the stimulating influence of a stamp club.

Undoubtedly you know several people—teachers scoutmasters, camp directors, etc.—who would be interested in starting a stamp club if they knew something about the great hobby of stamp collecting, and realised that it has many millions of followers the world over. Show them your *Wanderer Album*, and call their attention to this article. Many group leaders will welcome the idea of a stamp club, for it is both easy and inexpensive to organize, and it is sure to prove a lively, wholesome, and interest-arousing influence, wherever it may be.

A stamp club may be as formal or informal as you please. It can be started by saying, "Let's meet at George's house to-morrow night and swap stamps." At each meeting the date and place of the next meeting can be decided.

SUGGESTIONS FOR CLUB MEETINGS

Every club will naturally arrange its own programme to suit itself, and we offer the following remarks merely as suggestions to be adapted to your own plans.

Meetings should be held regularly, and for most clubs the best interval would seem to be every other week. If possible, the club should secure a permanent meeting place : perhaps a room in the local library, or a basement, attic, or garage donated by a member. If such a club room is not available, the meetings can be held in turn at the homes of the various members, where, by the way, some obliging wife or mother will usually be glad to serve at the appointed time that indispensable feature of all group meetings—the refreshments.

Fees for club members should be moderate : just enough to enable the club to subscribe to one or more stamp magazines, and to furnish (in the absence of the obliging wife or mother mentioned above) the "eats" for every meeting.

Never forget that the primary purpose of a stamp club is pleasure, and that anything which is disagreeable or boring to the majority of the members (long and dull speeches, for example) should be carefully avoided. Get the official business over as quickly as possible, and let the fun begin. Games, raffles, auctions, humorous speeches or articles, stamp treasure hunts, etc., will do infinitely more for a stamp club and its members than dragging out the dry-as-dust formalities of official business. Here are a few suggestions :—

Stamp Treasure Hunt : Packets of stamps are hidden in all parts of the room. Club members search for them, keeping what they find for their collection. Use some really good stamps and also, to create amusement, some utterly worthless ones.

Guessing Contest : A bowl of stamps is displayed, and each member writes a guess as to the number of stamps in the bowl. The person who makes the nearest guess wins the stamps. A lot of the cheapest stamps obtainable, with some good ones mixed in, is ideal for such a guessing contest.

Lucky Dip : Each person draws a stamp package, unseen, from a bag or box. Use really worthwhile "dips" and include one especially fine prize and one worthless "booby" prize. Wrap the

Newlands Road Philatelic Society (1953—67)
11) The beginnings

In the beginning was the stamp, and the stamp was with us, and the same was in the beginning with the stampede. All things collected were stamped upon our memories. In the stamp was all life, and all life was collected, and in the albums of life light shone from far off places, and nothing that was made was not displayed. And so it came to pass that the Newlands Road Philatelic Society was born, though in its infancy it was named the Stamp Club. (According to a letter from The Phillips.)

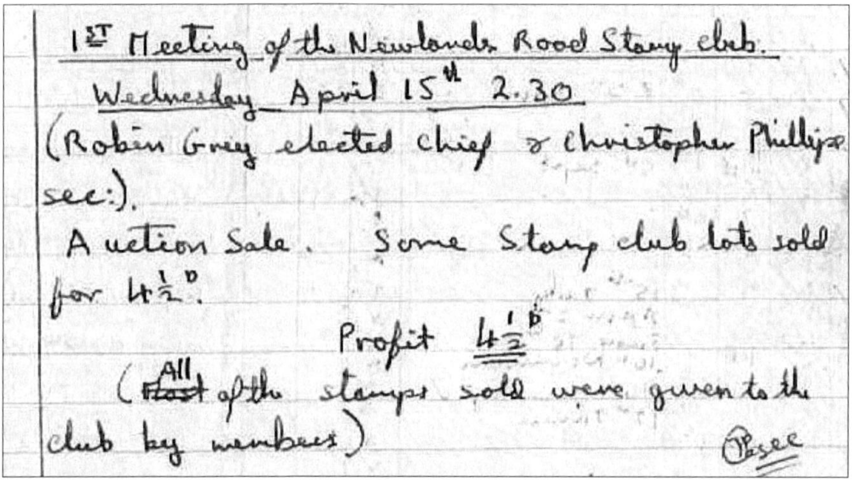
1ST Meeting of the Newlands Road Stamp club.
Wednesday April 15th 2.30
(Robin Grey elected chief & Christopher Phillips sec:).
Auction Sale. Some Stamp club lots sold for 4½D.
Profit 4½D
(~~Most~~ All of the stamps sold were given to the club by members)
CP sec

The above is a scan of the original minutes of the very first meeting. At first, meetings seemed to be held rather randomly. The 2nd one was only 5 days later, another auction sale; and the 3rd another 5 days later: we had a lucky dip, in which one paid 1½d each dip. During the week between the 4th and 5th meetings, members got some of their collections ready for a competition. The next door neighbour, Mr Hodgson, was asked to judge the 6 entries. He judged John Teasdale's the winner. Mr Hodgson was very generous and gave a prize of 2/6 to the top four. Colin Fowle was 2nd, and David and Christopher 3rd equal. Mrs Hodgson came to the 6th meeting and awarded the prizes. At that time we had 11 members: Robin Grey, (chief); Christopher Phillips (Secretary); Clive Grey; Colin Fowle; David Lloyd-Roberts; Christine Langridge (her name appears on the list, but I do not remember her ever attending); John Teasdale; Keith Spencer; Robert Holland, Malcolm Clift; and Brian Campsie.

Then, partly because of the Coronation party and summer holidays, no more stamp club meetings were held till October 3rd 1953.

I know I started an approval "service" to make money for the club. I bought large packets of stamps from Charles Lusted's shop (one of the two local stamp shops in town) for 2/6, and sold the stamps in approval books, mainly at The Skinners' School, but also to the members.

In the autumn of 1953 I was in the 4th year at school, and was now old enough to join the school stamp club. This met once a week, and I know I got some ideas of how better to run our club. Although we had kept records of all meetings, from now on the records were in more detail and more formal.

We may have had two meetings not recorded in between, because the Oct 3rd meeting was called meeting number 9. This was the second competition. The judges were Humphrey Smeeton and Bobby Ely, and the next meeting was another competition prize-giving. Eight members had entered; Robert was the winner and I was second. Some new members had joined: Peter Wells, his sister Wendy, and Peter Powell.

The following meeting was a treasure hunt, in which three members entered; all of them won prizes. We then seemed to have weekly meetings. All meetings were held in our dining room at number 15, except things like the treasure hunts (which were out-doors). The meetings seem to have had regular auctions and talks by myself and also quizzes.

Although a programme had been made up for April to July 1954, no June or July meetings took place. After the auction on 22nd of May, the next meeting was not till Nov 22nd. I do not re-call what happened then to have that break. Then we had another break from December 1954 to September 1955. From then on meetings were held more or less regularly till Autumn 1963.

Now the club was on a firmer footing, and a new chapter will deal with the rise of the club.

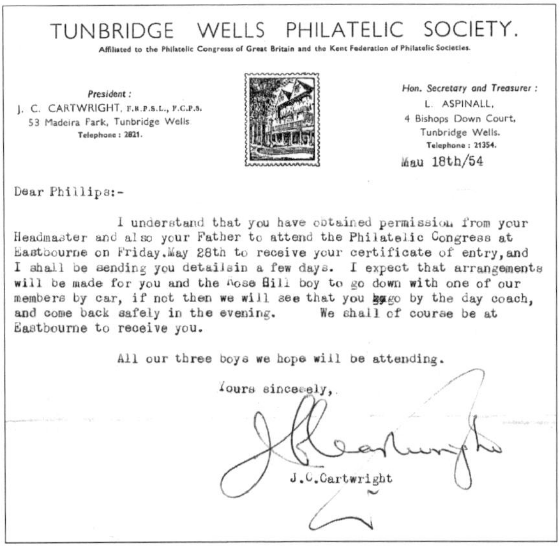

TUNBRIDGE WELLS PHILATELIC SOCIETY.

Affiliated to the Philatelic Congress of Great Britain and the Kent Federation of Philatelic Societies.

President :
J. C. CARTWRIGHT, F.R.P.S.L., F.C.P.S.
53 Madeira Park, Tunbridge Wells
Telephone : 2821.

Hon. Secretary and Treasurer :
L. ASPINALL,
4 Bishops Down Court,
Tunbridge Wells.
Telephone : 21354.

Mau 18th/54

Dear Phillips:-

I understand that you have obtained permission from your Headmaster and also your Father to attend the Philatelic Congress at Eastbourne on Friday.May 28th to receive your certificate of entry,and I shall be sending you detailsin a few days. I expect that arrangements will be made for you and the Rose Hill boy to go down with one of our members by car, if not then we will see that you go by the day coach, and come back safely in the evening. We shall of course be at Eastbourne to receive you.

All our three boys we hope will be attending.

Yours sincerely,

J.C.Cartwright

Through The Skinners' School stamp club I was entered into to the Tunbridge Wells PS annual Junior competition, and as the winner of my age group I was entered in 1954 into the national Melville Junior Stamp Competition, run by the Philatelic Congress of Great Britain. I did not win a cup or anything, but all entrants were awarded a certificate of Merit. That year's meeting was held in Eastbourne, and I and a boy from Rosehill School were given the day off school to be taken down by some members of the Tunbridge Wells Philatelic Society to accept our Certificates.

It was this, I believe, that spurred me on to get the Newlands club back on track.

One thing to remember is that at no time throughout its long life of 14 years did any adults have anything to do with the running of the club, and members who reached the age of 21 had to leave. We did ask a number of adults to help by judging competitions and giving talks. By September 1955 we had reached the 44th meeting. Average attendances were in the region of 5 to 8 members.

THE PHILATELIC CONGRESS OF GREAT BRITAIN

Certificate of Merit

awarded to

Christopher. J. Phillips.

for an entry in the

INTERMEDIATE CLASS

for the year

1954

Chairman
Executive Committee

Chairman
Competition Committee

MELVILLE MEMORIAL COMPETITION

12) New life and Prosperity from 1955

At the 45th meeting on 17 Sept 1955, we found ourselves without a President, because John Teasdale had moved to Sittingbourne. As a result Colin Fowle was elected President, and a programme was mapped out for the future, meeting mainly at fortnightly intervals. A competition was set, with the awards to be awarded at the 50th Meeting on 17 Dec 1955. We were lucky in that the Mayoress of the town accepted our invitation to present the prizes at that meeting. We had 3 judges: Bobby Ely, , myself as Secretary, and a non -collector, Mrs Jenkins. The overall winner was Virginia Timmis. Second was Peter Powell and third Simon Timmis. Only 10% marks separated the 10 contestants.

At the 48th meeting we had our first contact with the other all-Junior Stamp Club in the town, the Tudor Rose Stamp Club. They had three members and only one, Patrick Hoyte, was able to attend our meeting. Later all three decided to join us. By now we had

THIS IS A CERTIFICATE GIVEN
TO MEMBERS OF THE NEWLANDS
ROAD PHILATELIC SOCIETY FOR
GETTING A HIGH STANDARD
IN THE 50th MEETING AND 5th COMPETITION
(FOR OVER 50%)

Certificate of Merit

AWARDED TO
Peter Powell
ALSO RECEIVING 2nd PRIZE
FOR His ENTRY OF STAMPS
74¾ PERCENT
ON THE 17th DAY OF December 1955
GIVEN ON JUDGE'S APPROVAL:
C. J. Phillips
R. D. Ely

C.J. Phillips
Hon. Secretary of Society.

18 members.

At the 52nd meeting a few new ideas were suggested and agreed upon. We also started holding meetings in different members' homes, instead of only in my parents' dining room all the time.

Among the innovations were visits. We went to the local Post Office Sorting Office, to see how the mail was handled. Later, we were pleased that the local Kent and Sussex Courier were happy to show us around their printing works. We also visited a local Printing works in Tonbridge.

It was when the President of the Tunbridge Wells PS, Mr J C Cartwright, came to the Skinners' School PS that I asked him if he would come to give a talk to our Newlands Road club. I am so glad that I did, for I am sure that his accepting and encouraging us youngsters to be good collectors helped a great deal to make our club famous.

J. C. Cartwright (Jack) was a Canadian, living in Tunbridge Wells permanently, and was one of the rare signatories of the Roll of Distinguished Philatelists. He was actually added in 1956.

Mr Cartwright first attended our meetings on 11th Feb 1956. He gave us hints about entering the Melville Competition. Not only did he come, but several others came too. Two weeks later Miss N Brett did the same, and the following week Mr Brewer also came. Five of our members entered the Tunbridge Wells local competition to see who should be sent up to the national competition. Four of them won 1st, 2nd or 3rd prizes. Peter Powell was a winner in the youngest class C and was taken to Brighton to accept his certificate. Later we invited other members of the Tunbridge Wells Philatelic Society to give us some talks, to help us with entering competitions.

Rather than trying to tell the whole story in one long chapter, I am now going to split the chapters up into the various activities that the club did or took part in, but roughly in the order they were initiated.

13) Speakers
14) Newlands Post
15) Competitions
16) What Did We Do In Meetings
17) First Day Covers
18) Tunbridge Wells Hobbies Exhibition
19) Pictorials For a Brighter Britain Campaign
20) Press Coverage
21) Affiliations etc
22) 10th Anniversary
23) Main Members & Membership
24) Death Of NRPS & its Memories

Cake made by Mrs Powell, Peter's mother

13) Speakers

As stated in the previous chapter, our first speaker from outside the club was Mr J. C. Cartwright. Several members of the Tunbridge Wells club visited after that.

Mr J. C. Cartwright FRPS RDP
Miss N Brett
Mr Brewer
Mr Pearce
Mr Moat
Mr Reeves-Brown
Mr Maxwell

and Douglas Reed (12 Mount Zion, stamp shop).

All the above were from the Tunbridge Wells PS.

For our 100th meeting, the first national magazine editor presented the prizes and gave a talk. This was the first meeting I had to miss. I had the Asian Flu, and was in bed above the room where the meeting was taking place. (I believe I have a tape recording of this, somewhere in the mass of records I have kept.)

Mr Wilfrid B Haworth (Ed Stamp Collectors Fortnightly)
Kenneth Chapman (Ed Stamp Collecting Weekly)
James Watson (Assistant Ed Gibbon's Stamp Monthly)
Charles P Rang (Editor Gibbons Stamp monthly)
Cyril Harmer (Harmers Auctions)
Mr Brown (Stamp Designer for Harrison & Sons - The British stamp printers for the UK Post Office)
Mr Toms (MBE) PC of GB

(All the above came to the annual meeting for competition awards)

In addition we had the following come to our meetings to talk to us.

B. C. Allcock from Croydon
Ian T Hamilton (Epsom)
Ian Ash (Brighton)

Tom Morgan (Ed Philatelic Magazine)
Dr Gordon Ward
Mr O. W. Newport (Assist Ed Stamp collecting)

Up until and including the 100th meeting, most

Mr Muffett Mayor - Colin Fowle

Mr Muffett Mayor - Peter Lewis

Colin Fowle, David Reich Mr WB Haworth, Patrick H yte

Peter Powell - Kenneth Chapman

James Watson - Christopher Selmes

C. P Rang - Simon Levett

Cyril Harmer - Patrick Smith

Cyril Harmer - Peter Powell Susan Smith

Shirley Burr David Green
Mr Thoms - Peter Powell Graham Edwards

Chris Phillips, R.C Emery & J C Cartwright at the 10th Anniversary Exhibition

meetings were held in my parents' dining room, or in a few of the other members' homes. This practice continued after that as well, except when we had the important speakers above. Then we hired a room at Culverden Hall. For the special meetings we usually invited the Tunbridge Wells PS members along as well. Parents of members were also invited.

14) The Newlands Post

In the 4th year of the club, we decided to have a newsletter. David Lloyd Roberts was elected editor, assisted by Susan Smith. That was in 1956. It was originally intended as an annual magazine.

Now imagine, we needed 20 copies for members and advertising etc. We had no printing machine and

THE NEWLANDS ROAD PHUILATELIC SOCIETY'S YEARLY MAGAZINE.
THE NEWLANDS ROAD POST 1956 17

Editor:- DAVID L-ROBERTS. Wendy Walls
Vice Editor:- SUSAN SMITH.
NO: 1. Volume 1. 4th year of club price 4d

1) EDITORIAL

To begin our yearly magasine we are sure all members would like to congratulate those who entered the junior Melville Memorial Competition 5 members entered,4 of them won prizes.In class C(juniors) Peter Powell was Ist (7/-6D);Susan Smith 2nd (5/-);in the class B(intermediate) Patrick Hoyte was / 3rd(2/-6d);in class A(seniors) Christopher Phillips was 2nd (5/-).Peter Powell will also have a day at Brighton and a certificate of Merit and may win £2 or £1.

Before we go any Further we would like to remind you of past events.

The first meeting was held at 15 Newlands Roade on the 15th of april 1953, with 5 members present at the auction which brought in4½ for the club funds. On the ~~6th May~~ 10th of May 1953 we ~~has~~ had our first competition Mr. Hodgeson gave prizes to the value of 10/-, John Teasdale was first(2/-6d)

Last August 1955 ourPresedent unfortunatly had to move to Sittingbourne. And Colin Fowle was elected President.On December the 17th the Mayoress of Royal Tunbridge Wells,presented the prizes of our 50th meeting

~~competition,Virginia Timmis won first prize. We have also been very to~~
~~Happy have Mr~~

competitionVirginia Timmis won first prize. We have also been very happy to have Mr. CartwrighB, president of the Tunbridge Wells Philatelic soiciety, Miss Brett,Mr. Brewer,and Mr.PEARCE of the Tunbridge Wells Philatelic Soiciety to visit,help and talk to us

This year 9 of our members entered the Tunbridge Wells Hobbies Exibition with their stamps,Christopher Phillips won 3rd Prize in the Open class,and Colin Fowle had a Highly Commended in the children's class.

Here are the results of this years elections,held in April:-

PRESIDENT:- Colin Fowle
Vice President:- Virginia Timmis
SECRETARY:- Christopher Phillips
Vice Secretary:- Peter Powell
TREASURER:- Christopher Phillips
LIBRARIAN:- Peter Powell .
EDITOR:- David Lloyd-Roberts
Vice Editor:- Susan Smith

It was also voted for a subscription of 1/- per year for every member and for1/-3 for those who borrow CLUB books,TO BE PAID BEFORE K OCTOBERTHE IST 1956.

two of us could type (well just about - I am still a one finger typist). No, we did not type out 20 copies separately, we did have carbon papers. And I laboriously typed it 4 times, making 16 copies, and David typed it once, making the last four copies. There were 4 pages,

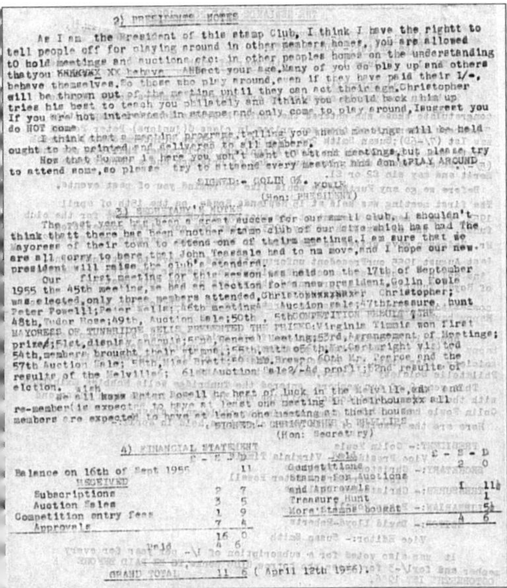

2) PRESIDENT'S NOTES

As I am the President of this stamp Club, I think I have the rightt to tell people off for playing around in other members homes, you are allowed tO hold meetings and auctions etc: in other peoples homes on the understanding thatyou XX behave Act your age. Many of you do play up and others behave themselves. So those who play around, even if they have paid their 1/-, will be thrown out of the meeting until they can act their age. Christopher tries his best to teach you philately and Ithink you should back him up If you are not interested in stamps and only come to play around, Isuggest you do NOT come

I think that a meeting programme, telling you when meetings will be held ought to be printed and delivered to all members.

Now that Summer is here you won't want tO attend meetings, but please try to attend some, so please try to attend every meeting and don't PLAY AROUND

SIGNED:- COLIN G. FOWLE
(Hon: PRESIDENT)

3) SECRETARY'S NOTES

The past year has been a great succes for our small club, I shouldn't think thatt there has been another stamp club of our size which has had The Mayoress of their town to attend one of theirs meetings. I am sure that we are all sorry to here that John Teasdale had to move, and I hope our new president will raise the club's standard.

Our first meeting for this season was held on the 17th of September 1955 the 45th meeting, we had an election for a new president, Colin Fowle was elected, only three members attended, Christopher; 46th meeting Auction sale; 47th treasure hunt Peter Powell; Peter Wells; 48th, Tudor Rose; 49th, Auction Sale; 50th, 5th COMPETITION RESULT THE MAYORESS OF TUNBRIDGE WELLS PRESENTED THE PRIZES: Virginia Timmis won first prize; 51st, display [illegible]; 52nd, General Meeting; 53rd, Arrangement of Meetings; 54th, members brought their stamps; 55th, [illegible] 56th, Mr. Cartwright visited 57th Auction Sale; 58th, Miss Brett; 59th, Mr. Brewer 60th Mr. Pearce and the results of the Melville; 61st Auction Sale 2/-4d profit; 62nd results of election.

We all wish Peter Powell the best of luck in the Melville, All members are expected to have at least one meeting at their house

SIGNED:- CHRISTOPHER J. PHILLIPS
(Hon: Secretary)

4) FINANCIAL STATEMENT

	£ - s - d		Paid	£ - s - D
Balance on 16th of Sept 1955	11		Competitions	2 0
RECEIVED			Stamps for Auctions and Approvals	1 11½
Subscriptions	2 7		Treasure Hunt	1
Auction Sales	3 5		More Stamps bought	5½
Competition entry fees	1 9			4 6
Approvals	7 4			
	16 0			
Paid	4 6			
GRAND TOTAL	11 6 (April 12th 1956).			

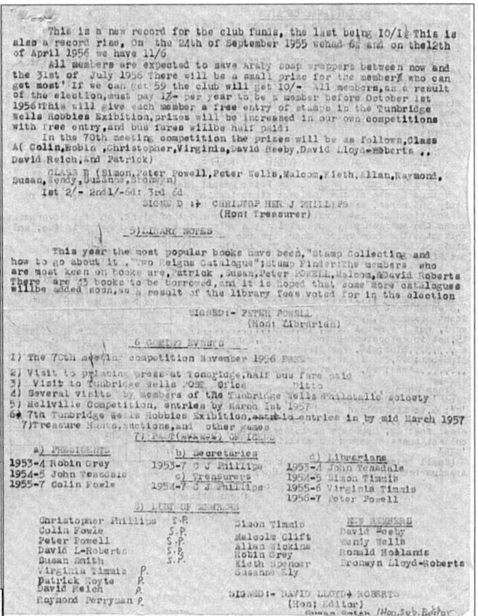

This is a new record for the club funds, the last being 10/1½ This is also a record rise, On the 24th of September 1955 wehad 6½ and on the12th of April 1956 we have 11/6

All members are expected to save Araby soap wrappers between now and the 31st of July 1956 There will be a small prize for the member who can get most' If we can get 59 the club will get 10/- All members, as a result of the election, must pay 1/- per year to be a member before October 1st 1956: This will give each member a free entry of stamps in the Tunbridge Wells Hobbies Exibition, prizes will be increased in our own competitions with free entry, and bus fares willbe half paid:

In the 70th meeting competition the prizes will be as follows, Class A(Colin, Robin, Christopher, Virginia, David Beeby, David Lloyd-Roberts, David Reich, And Patrick)

CLASS B (Simon, Peter Powell, Peter Wells, Malcom, Kieth, Allan, Raymond, Susan, Wendy, Suzanne, Bronwyn)

1st 2/- 2nd 1/-6d: 3rd 6d

SIGNED :- CHRISTOPHER J PHILLIPS
(Hon: Treasurer)

5) LIBRARY NOTES

This year the most popular books have been, "Stamp Collecting and how to go about it", "Two Reigns Catalogue"; Stamp Finder: The members who are most keen on books are, Patrick, Susan, Peter POWELL, Malcom, & David Roberts There are 43 books to be borrowed, and it is hoped that some more catalogues willbe added soon, as a result of the library fees voted for in the election

SIGNED:- PETER POWELL
(Hon: Librarian)

6 COMING EVENTS

1) The 70th meeting competition November 1956 [illegible]
2) Visit to printing press at Tonbridge, half bus fare paid
3) Visit to Tunbridge Wells POST Office Ditto
4) Several visits by members of the Tunbridge Wells Philatelic Society
5) Melville Competition, entries by March 1st 1957
6) 7th Tunbridge Wells Hobbies Exibition, entries in by mid March 1957
7) Treasure Hunts, auctions, and other games

7) PAST(MEMBERS) OFFICERS

a) PRESIDENTS	b) Secretaries	d) Librarians
1953-4 Robin Grey	1953-7 C J Phillips	1953-4 John Teasdale
1954-5 John Teasdale	c) Treasurers	1954-5 Simon Timmis
1955-7 Colin Fowle	1954-7 C J Phillips	1955-6 Virginia Timmis
		1956-7 Peter Powell

8) LIST OF MEMBERS

			NEW MEMBERS
Christopher Phillips	S.P.	Simon Timmis	David Beeby
Colin Fowle	S.P.	Malcolm Clift	Wendy Wells
Peter Powell	S.P.	Allan Wickins	Ronald Hollands
David L-Roberts	S.P.	Robin Grey	Bronwyn Lloyd-Roberts
Susan Smith	S.P.	Kieth Spencer	
Virginia Timmis	P.	Susanne Ely	
Patrick Hoyte	P.		
David Reich	P.		
Raymond Perryman	P.		

SIGNED:- DAVID LLOYD-ROBERTS
(Hon: Editor)
Susan Smith (Hon.Sub.Editor)

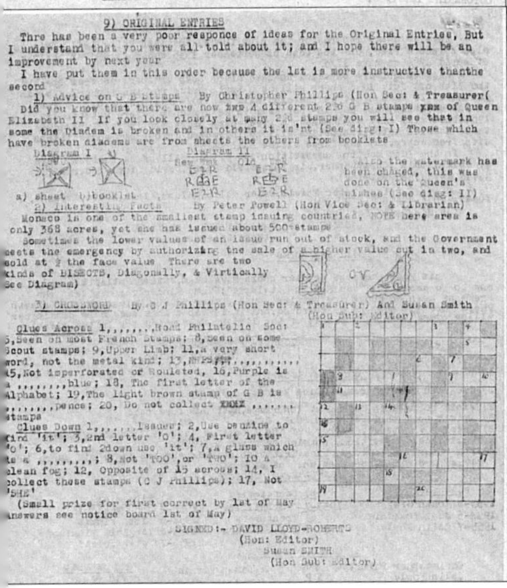

9) ORIGINAL ENTRIES

Thre has been a very poor responce of ideas for the Original Entries, But I understand that you were all told about it; and I hope there will be an improvement by next year

I have put them in this order because the 1st is more instructive thanthe second

1) Advice on G B Stamps By Christopher Phillips (Hon Sec: & Treasurer(

Did you know that there are now 4 different 2½d G B stamps of Queen Elizabeth II If you look closely at many 2½d stamps you will see that in some the Diadem is broken and in others it is'nt (See diag: I) Those which have broken diadems are from sheets the others from booklets

Diagram I — a) sheet b) booklet

Diagram II — New Wmk, Old Wmk

Also the watermark has been chaged, this was done on the Queen's wishes (See diag: II)

2) Interesting Facts By Peter Powell (Hon Vice Sec: & Librarian)

Monaco is one of the smallest stamp issuing countries, NOTE here area is only 368 acres, yet she has issued about 500 stamps

Sometimes the lower values of an issue run out of stock, and the Government meets the emergency by authorizing the sale of a higher value cut in two, and sold at ½ the face value There are two kinds of BISECTS, Diagonally, & Virtically See Diagram)

3) CROSSWORD By C J Phillips (Hon Sec: & Treasurer) And Susan Smith (Hon Sub: Editor)

Clues Across 1,,,,,,,,Royal Philatelic Soc: 5,Seen on most French Stamps; 8,Seen on some Scout stamps; 9,Upper Limb; 11,a very short word, not the metal kind; 13,,,,,,,,,,,,,, 15,Not imperforated or Rouletted, 16,Purple is a ,,,,,,,,,blue; 18, The first letter of the Alphabet; 19,The light brown stamp of G B is ,,,,,,,,pence; 20, Do not collect ,,,,,,,, stamps

Clues Down 1,,,,,,,Issues; 2,Use beauline to find 'it'; 3,2nd letter 'O'; 4, First letter 'O'; 6,to find 2down use 'it'; 7,A glass which is a ,,,,,,,,,,; 8,Not 'TOO',or 'TWO'; 10 A clean fog; 12, Opposite of 15 across; 14, I collect these stamps (C J Phillips); 17, Not 'SHE'

(Small prize for first correct by 1st of May answers see notice board 1st of May)

SIGNED:- DAVID LLOYD-ROBERTS
(Hon: Editor)
Susan SMITH
(Hon Sub: Editor)

so that was a lot of typing, and drawing of crosswords etc. (The typing errors showed!)

For issue number two, a friend gave us a small A5 size hand-held duplicator. So issue number two was like a little booklet on 19 pages (20 was blank) and was issued in May 1967. See next page for the cover

THE NEWLANDS POST.

No: 2. Vol: 2.
The Newlands Road Philatelic Society's Annual Magazine.

Price, FOURPENCE.
Reprinted. May 1957

A.. Members Edition.
EDITOR:- PATRICK HOYTE.
Sub. Editor:- DAVID BEEBY.

EDITORIAL.
Here are the results of the annual General Election.
PRESIDENT:- Colin Fowle.
Vice:- Susan Smith & David L -R.
SECRETARY:- Christopher Phillips.
Vice:- Peter Powell.
TREASURER:- Christopher Phillips.
LIBRARIAN:- Peter Powell.
EDITOR & Sub. Editor, see above.
Auctioneer:- Colin Fowle.
It was decided at a recent meeting that Alan Wickens should be banned from the Society for one year. Patrick Hoyte was awarded his Silver Privilege, and Peter Veness his Privilege.
Our thanks are due to Mr. J.C. Cartwright for the way in which he has helped the club in the past year,

page. Sadly I have lost the next 2 issues. I cannot find copies anywhere. An interesting article in no. 2 was by David Beeby (son of the Skinners' School Headmaster) when we went on our first visit to London. Part of that is published below.

Each edition had the officers' reports and the financial accounts, as well reports on meetings and competition successes by members in local and national competitions. By issue number 5, we had been given permission to have the newsletter run off on the Skinners' School duplicator. It was now a Foolscap size and had 10 pages, partly financed by adverts from the two local stamp shops, and even by a few members. Another innovation was the addition of a stuck-on print of a photo of Peter Powell

VISIT TO LONDON.
(By David Beeby).
On Jan [illegible], a party of 5 members visited London. After meeting at Caring Cross at 9.20 am., we walked along the Strand where there are numerous stamps shops including S.G. We then made our way to the publishing office of 'STAMP COLLECTING' in Malden Lane, the main object of our visit.
The Editor Mr. Chapman kindly explained the work which goes into compiling the articals for each edition. He then took us to the printing works and Mr. Hodgson, the director, took us round his factory & showed us how a kind of typewriter punches holes into spools of paper, which, when fed into a monotype machine automatically arranged the type. We also saw to our great interest, the blocks depicting the stamps on the paper. After the printing we saw the folding, cutting and stitching of the paper. Mr. Hodgson kindly gave us some stamps and a free copy of 'STAMP COLLECTING' afterwards.
Next we went by bus to the British Museum, where we found the collection of Victorian stamps which we found very interesting. After we had disposed of our packed lunches, we decided, after some debate, to go to a Magic shop and then to a News Cinema before rourning Home. We are very

NEWLANDS POST. 6d.

Vol.3. No. 2. (Whole No. 5). Price 6d.

Published by the Junior NEWLANDS ROAD PHILATELIC SOCIETY.
Printed by Christopher Phillips on the Skinners' School duplicator, very kindly lent by the Headmaster, Mr. C.H. Beeby M.A.

Society affiliated to:- "THE PHILATELIC CONGRESS OF GREAT BRITAIN". "THE BRITISH PHILATELIC ASSOCIATION".
And members of:- "THE WORLD ASSOCIATION OF YOUNG STAMP COLLECTORS"
Published January 1959.

THE 135TH. MEETING, 27th SEPTEMBER 1958.

At this meeting we were very lucky to have KENNETH CHAPMAN, Editor of "STAMP COLLECTING" to present the prizes of the "NEWLANDS STAMP" competition & to give us a talk and display.

After the usual business had been attended to (here we decided to become affiliated to the PHILATELIC CONGRESS OF GREAT BRITAIN), Mr. Chapman presented the prizes as follows:-

The "NEWLANDS STAMP". :- Peter Powell (see above Photograph).
CLASS A. 1st. Christopher Phillips & Patrick Hoyte. 3/9 (each) 68%
2nd. David Beeby. 2/- 64½%
4th. Christopher Selmes. 1/6 66½%
CLASS B. 1st. Peter Powell. 5/- 71½%
2nd. David Taylor. 2/6 61%
3rd. Bronwen Phillips. 2/- 60%
Best New Member:- Simon Levett (Pocket book of stamps given by the "W.A.Y.S.C."). 62½%
Good try by youngest member:- Margaret Collier (⊞ Canadian new stamps given by Mr. Cartwright.) 50%

ALL other entrants received consolation prizes of 15 covers.

This year a record of 19 members entered, we also had a record attendance of 19 members and 2 visitors at this meeting (Miss N. Brett was the other visitor, representing the Tunbridge Wells P.S.)

Mr. Chapman then gave his talk and display, entitled "INFORMAL PHILATELY", which was a well got together display ranging from "Love Letters" to "Sperati Forgeries". We were very grateful indeed to have such a distinguished speaker, writer, broadcaster and T.V. "Star" down from London specially to give our small junior society this most interesting lecture.

EDITORIAL.

Well, here we are again with another "NEWLANDS POST", and what a wonderful value you are getting for your money, because this one is illustrated (Thank you Colin). What a lot of changes have taken place since I last wrote. We now rejoice in a new secretary, Peter Powell, who is at present managing very well (with the help of his mother) and with your respect and support, he should be a success, and also a new Treasurer who, we hope, is also managing. We must, of course, say how sorry we are that Christopher is unable to carry on as Secretary and Treasurer, for without him this club would not exist; he has been the live-wire throughout our history and is still giving a lot of extremely valuable assistance. The membership too is increasing, and soon we shall have to stop admitting new members or we shall be overstepping our limit of fifty. It is a pity though that only about thirty per cent

receiving the annual trophy, “The Newlands Stamp”, from Kenneth Chapman, Editor of “Stamp Collecting Weekly” at the 135th meeting (Sept 1958). Issue num-

NEWLANDS POST. 6D

Published by the NEWLANDS ROAD PHILATELIC SOCIETY.
July 1959. Price 6d.
Vol. 4 No. 1. (Whole No 6).

Printed by Christopher Phillips on the Skinners' School duplicator, kindly lent by the Headmaster, Mr. C H. Beeby M.A.

Society Affiliated to:-
"THE PHILATELIC CONGRESS OF GREAT BRITAIN", "THE BRITISH PHILATELIC ASSOCIATION" and "THE WORLD ASSOCIATION OF YOUNG STAMP COLLECTORS".

GREAT SUCCESS FOR OUR STAND AT THE TUNBRIDGE WELLS HOBBIES EXHIBITION, APRIL 1st – 4th 1959.

Photograph of our stand as seen from the main entrance of the Assembly Hall Tunbridge Wells.

In spite of the exhibition being open for a day and a half less than last year many more people took a keen interest in our stand. This interest was due to advance publicity of our stand in four national philatelic magazines, several 'B.P.A.' posters in the local schools and stamp shops, the various competitions, and the new electrical quiz (made by Malcolm Clift). Mr H. J. Wallace of the B.P.A. Council personally congratulated us and said that he would like to see the local society putting on displays such as ours.

ber 6 also had a photo; this time it was of our first stall at the Annual Tunbridge Wells Hobbies Exhibition in the Assembly Hall. It was now 1959. From now on our membership was growing from just Newlands Road and the near by roads, to all Tunbridge Wells, and even beyond.

Also by now we were affiliated to three national organisations:

The British Philatelic Association

The World Association of Young Stamp Collectors

The Philatelic Congress Of Great Britain. (We were the only all junior club to join.)

We could now send our own entries to the Melville competition. So our members had two chances, us and the TWPS.

Issue Number 7 is also sadly missing from my

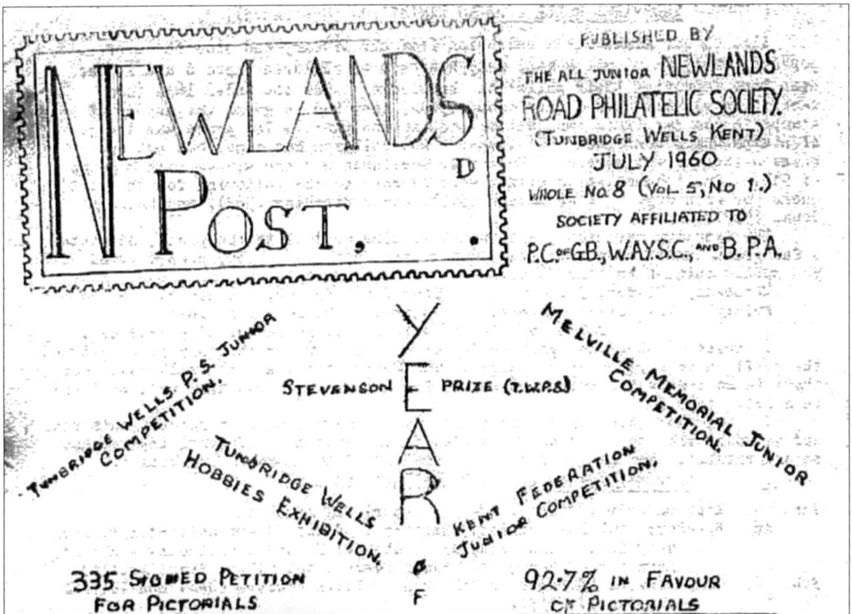

NEWLANDS POST. D

PUBLISHED BY THE ALL JUNIOR NEWLANDS ROAD PHILATELIC SOCIETY. (TUNBRIDGE WELLS KENT) JULY 1960 WHOLE No. 8 (VOL. 5, No 1.) SOCIETY AFFILIATED TO P.C. OF GB., W.A.Y.S.C., AND B. P.A.

YEAR OF WIN

TUNBRIDGE WELLS P.S. JUNIOR COMPETITION.

STEVENSON PRIZE (T.W.P.S.)

MELVILLE MEMORIAL JUNIOR COMPETITION.

TUNBRIDGE WELLS HOBBIES EXHIBITION.

KENT FEDERATION JUNIOR COMPETITION.

335 SIGNED PETITION FOR PICTORIALS

92·7% IN FAVOUR OF PICTORIALS

NEW HONORARY MEMBER ELECTED.
No. 84 Christopher Phillips, 15, Newlands Road, Tun. Wells.

collection.

Number 8 (10 full pages) celebrated a year of winners. It was 1960, and during 1959 we had started our Campaign For Small Pictorial Postage Stamps (as can be seen on this front page, and in a special chapter devoted to this campaign). We also found out how to put photos directly into the stencil to print in one go. Sadly the front page photo didn't work, but the other

Christopher Phillips, transferred to Honorary membership.

HONORARY MEMBER

H4. Christopher Phillips. I am sure that no person has done more for this society than Christopher Phillips. For 5½ years he was our secretary, ½ year Vice President, and 1 year our President. Through Christopher's inspiration, encouragement and help to all its members, particularly the junior ones, the Society has become what it is now. I think All that we can say is a very warm "Thank you Christopher". Christopher is also a honorary member and Vice President of the W.A.Y.S.C., and a member of the T.W.P.S.

Above, on Page Three: I had now grown too old to be a member. But we did have a few other adult Honorary members and so I was asked to join them. All had been helpful to the club.

NEWLANDS POST. 4D.

JANUARY 1961. Whole Number 9 Vol. 5. No. 2.

EDITORIAL

The thanks of the society are due to many people, - members' parents for allowing meetings to be held at their homes (and providing refreshments and transport) - visiting speakers and prize presenters. Special thanks to Mr. Rang, also to Christopher and Magnus Samuel (who came at short notice) to whom we apologise for the small attendance.

Contributions are always hard to find but this time the task has been very difficult. Only one member (Hamish Kirk, a postal member) sent in a contribution without being personally asked!!! It seems that more would notice, or even care if the magazine was written entirely by Christopher and one or two others.

Some members may or may not know about the proposed Social Club - details are to be found elsewhere in this issue, please let us have your views on this.

Let us hope 1961 will be as successful a year for the N.R.P.S. as was 1960. As I said in my last Editorial, It'S up to you.

pages were quite good.

For issue number 9 we changed the format to half foolscap, and we only had 16 half pages. The stories included a report by my sister, Bronwen, on our visit to London to be shown round Stanley Gibbons, their new issue dept and the rare stamps room, behind solid steel doors!! We had been shown round by James Watson, Assistant Editor of Gibbon's Stamp Monthly.

Issue no 10 (and all the following issues) reverted to the foolscap size. On this issue (being the 10th) we

NEWLANDS POST 6d.

No. 10 (Vol. 6, No. 1). TUNBRIDGE WELLS. JULY 1961

EDITORIAL

EDITOR:- DAVID REICH (All correspondence concerning this magazine should be addressed to:- "Croylands", 165 St Johns Road, Tunbridge Wells.)

HOBBIES EXHIBITION

Our stand this year was the best we have had, in lay-out and in position, we were right next to the main entrance, and were again very priviledged to have the use of a

reproduced the very first issue over 4 pages, from the original Quarto size. We now were getting advertising from the famous WEEKS departmental store as well as the stamp shops and L Reich & Sons, the jewellers. Well

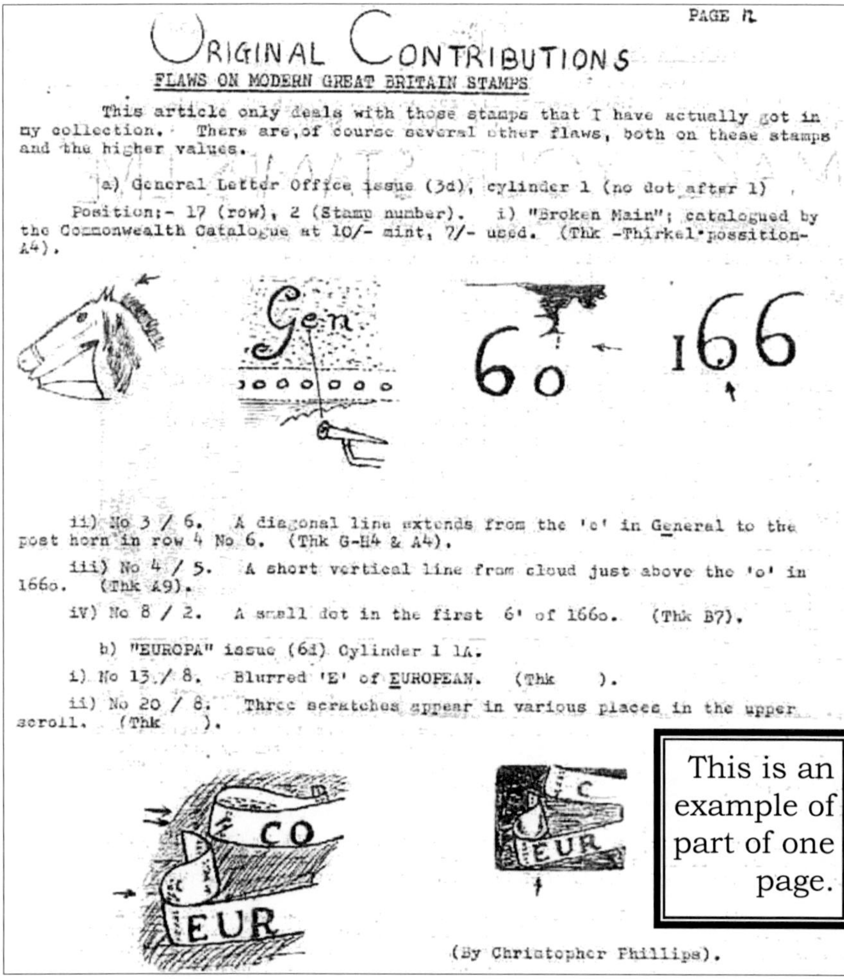

PAGE 12

ORIGINAL CONTRIBUTIONS

FLAWS ON MODERN GREAT BRITAIN STAMPS

This article only deals with those stamps that I have actually got in my collection. There are, of course several other flaws, both on these stamps and the higher values.

a) General Letter Office issue (3d), cylinder 1 (no dot after 1)

Position:- 17 (row), 2 (Stamp number). i) "Broken Main"; catalogued by the Commonwealth Catalogue at 10/- mint, 7/- used. (Thk -Thirkel possition-A4).

ii) No 3 / 6. A diagonal line extends from the 'e' in General to the post horn in row 4 No 6. (Thk G-H4 & A4).

iii) No 4 / 5. A short vertical line from cloud just above the 'o' in 1660. (Thk A9).

iv) No 8 / 2. A small dot in the first 6' of 1660. (Thk B7).

b) "EUROPA" issue (6d) Cylinder 1 1A.

i) No 13 / 8. Blurred 'E' of EUROPEAN. (Thk).

ii) No 20 / 8. Three scratches appear in various places in the upper scroll. (Thk).

(By Christopher Phillips).

This is an example of part of one page.

their son was the Editor by now.

Thanks to the hard work of David Green and Peter Powell, they had arranged to have social meetings after every other meeting, with all sorts of games available and even films, but so few took it up that it had to be cancelled. Hence the big headline in issue no 11 (Feb 1962).

NEWLANDS POST 6d.

No. 11 (Vol 6, No 2) TUNBRIDGE WELLS FEBURARY 1962

IT'S YOUR OWN

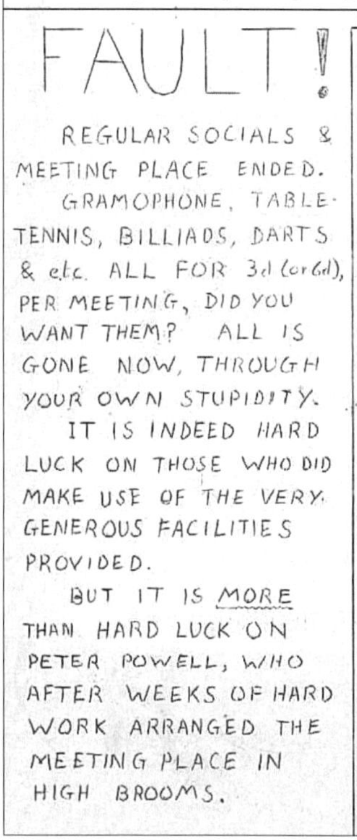

FAULT!

REGULAR SOCIALS & MEETING PLACE ENDED.

GRAMOPHONE, TABLE-TENNIS, BILLIADS, DARTS & etc. ALL FOR 3d (or 6d), PER MEETING, DID YOU WANT THEM? ALL IS GONE NOW, THROUGH YOUR OWN STUPIDITY.

IT IS INDEED HARD LUCK ON THOSE WHO DID MAKE USE OF THE VERY GENEROUS FACILITIES PROVIDED.

BUT IT IS MORE THAN HARD LUCK ON PETER POWELL, WHO AFTER WEEKS OF HARD WORK ARRANGED THE MEETING PLACE IN HIGH BROOMS.

In August 1962, the 12th Newlands Post headlined the coming 10th Anniversary of the club for 1963.

From the 5th anniversary onwards, the club celebrated its birthday on April 15th 1953 with a party and a birthday cake, which, if my memory holds true, was made by Mrs Powell (Peter's mum). But for the 10th anniversary, something bigger was planned.

Not only was the club unique in that it was an all junior one, only ever run by non adults (in those days one did not become adult till 21), but it was accepted for affiliation to national adult societies and now was about to celebrate 10 years of

No. 12. (Vol 7, No I) TUNBRIDGE WELLS. AUGUST 1962

TENTH ANNIVERSARY N.R.P.S. 15th APRIL 1963 —

EDI

EDITOR:-
DAVID REICH
"Croylands",
165, St. John's Rd.
TUNBRIDGE WELLS,
Kent.

Special Exhibition?

Next year will be an unique occasion in the history of philately, 'the sole example of SELF-RUN junior societies' • will be celebrating its TENTH ANNIVERSARY.

activity.

Not all the stuff in the Newlands Post was of a serious nature. Here is one such article!

COTTON REELS.
Rather bulky - not a very collectable item.

ORIGINALS (Continued)

CUT SQUARE. PHILATELIC TERMS (Redescribed) (Continued)
A drunken hater of modern issues.

FLY SPECKS.
Glasses used by insects to inspect newly printed stamps, usually found stuck to stamps on the most unusual places - invisible to sane collectors.

IMPERFORATED
Stamps with their perforations cut off (or filled in) to make a rarity.

POACHED EGG.
Fried stamps.

LETTERPRESS.
Often used by the G.P.O. to flatten thick letters.

(To be concluded next Newlands Post)

+=====+

The Post was now being printed on a duplicator owned by the parents of one of the members (Margaret Collier), instead of the Skinners' School, as I was now

at The Medway College Of Technology, studying for my BSc.

The 13th issue was much smaller than had been produced before, as I and the editor were too busy at the time and Peter Powell produced a 4 page version, looking forward to the 10th Anniversary Exhibition, which was to be the biggest issue ever, and had another innovation. As usual there were reports of past meetings and the future programme.

Interestingly, at the October meeting, to present the annual awards we were privileged to have Mr Brown from Harrison & Sons, the UK Stamp printing firm. He brought with him a film on stamp printing. 15 Members and 8 visitors were told all about printing postage stamps by this famous printers' from High Wycombe.

Socials were now back on the agenda, and these meetings were held in the High Brooms Youth Centre, after alternate meetings.

The annual January visit to London took place as usual when 7 members went to some interesting places like Madame Tussaud's and the planetarium, and Lyons Corner House (for breakfast!)

236

10th ANNIVERSARY 6d

EXHIBITION
ISSUE
OF

No. 14.

JULY 20th 1963

TUNBRIDGE WELLS KENT.

PUBLISHED BY THE ONLY ALL JUNIOR PHILATELIC SOCIETY IN EXISTANCE, THE

NEWLANDS ROAD PHILATELIC SOCIETY

1953 - 1963

INDEX

The N.R.P.S. is indeed most grateful to all the above advertisers, and we hope that readers will patronise all or some of them. It is to be noted that Weekes' front window displays have been decorated with enlarged photographs of European stamps, this we think is very effective.

Then came the BIG ISSUE, number 14, for the Public Exhibition opened officially by the Mayor in the Art Club Rooms on the famous Pantiles.

YES the latest innovation was adding COLOUR to the front page. Two printings of page one had to be made, the black print on a Gestetner machine, and the colour on a Banda machine. We had 250 copies printed. There were 16 pages, including a plan of the exhibition, adverts from Harringtons at “5 Ways”, Premier Health Food Stores, Binns Corner House (the Pantiles), Weeks Departmental Stores, Fox Brothers & Gladys Wells (Pantiles) Jupp & Sons (Fudge Makers, Pantiles) Hall’s Bookshop, The Stamp Shop (D Read) and Charles A Lusted. More about this exhibition will come in its own chapter.

This edition also had an article about how the GPO had given way to 8/9 of our demands!

Sadly, there were only to be two more editions:

Issue number 15. Published 1st January 1964.

EDITORIAL

EDITOR:
David Green,
69, Nursery Road,
High Brooms,
Tunbridge Wells,
Kent.

I am editor of this magazine. Or at least I
thought I was when I took over this office.
But now I am not quite so sure. Why? Well
how can the editor be editor when there is
nothing to be edited! Of course I can always
rely on people like Peter Powell and Chris
Phillips who can always be called upon to write
an article for the N.P. and it is fairly easy to get the yearly
reports from the various officers after a little persuasion but the
vast majority of the membership never get anything in print, not
because they cannot but because they will not. I sympathize with those
people who have examinations at school and all the rest of it but I
cannot believe that these people can never find half an hour to write
... read something from the

NEWLANDS POST SPECIAL 1°

Tunbridge Wells, August 1966. SPECIAL TWO PAGE EDITION. No. 16
The Magazine of the NEWLANDS ROAD PHILATELIC SOCIETY, the ONLY all JUNIOR Society,

YES! IT'S BACK AGAIN.

EDITORIAL

Well, it's here again, after more than two years absence, the NEWLANDS POST is once more in print and although it has only two sides, a far cry from the mamoth 16 page 10th anniversary issue of 1963, I feel sure that in the future it will be able to regain its original size and popularity. This is to be my last editorial although my successor has not yet been appointed and we are badly in need of someone to fill this very important (newlands) post. The history of the society will be new to few of our readers and whilst the past two years have not been our best, I feel sure that in the not too distant future the society will once again have a moderately sized and active membership.

My best wishes go to Andrew Crighton, our new secretary and also a completely new member, to Robert Romer, our new Chairman and to Graham Camfield, the new Treasurer and also to the other committee members.

(Dave Green)
Editor (Past President)

Secreatry's Report

A meeting was held on 30th July for the purpose of bringing in new members and forming a new committee. Four new members were enrolled; Beverly and Jennifer Kershaw, Malcolm Lawrence and Gary Parker.

An enjoyable evening was spent watching slides shown by Chris Phillips about the society. This was followed by an auction and the new committee was elected.

This meeting was followed by a further meeting the following Saturday, an auction was also held at this. Although the attendance at these two meetings shows some improvement on some of the past meetings there is still a long way to go before the attendance justifies inviting a speaker from any distance to the meetings. But the recent increase does give a real hope for a substantial rise in new members.

Andrew Crighton, Hon. Secretary.

President's Report

I would first like to say how honoured I am to be your new President, although the election took place in my absence. However, I must admit that when I joined way back in April 1961 I certainly did not think that I would ever become President. Moreover I now hope that the club, now in its fourteenth year will become as strong as it has ever been but all depends on members' support. It is now up to members to try to attend meetings regularly, to introduce new members and to give full support to the committee.

I also hope that the campaign will not have proved a waste of time since the success of the club (and indeed its ability to continue) depends on the number of members.

Robert Romer
President.

Treasurer's Report

An auction sale held during the meeting on 30th July in the Tunbridge Wells Art Club rooms resulted in raising over 25/- for club funds.

Another auction held on 6th August raised 3/3 for club funds.

The committee has decided that subscriptions should remain as usual this year, that is to say 1/9 for junior members and 2/6 for senior members. Subscriptions will be collected in the near future.

Graham Camfield
Hon. Treasurer.

THE NEWLANDS STAMP

This is the trophy awarded every year in the club's annual competition.

There are two classes (Junior & Senior) and usually 6 to 8 prizes.

Start preparing your entry NOW.

Number 15 on Jan 1st 1964, and in August 1966 the 16th. The whole of the front page can be seen on the previous page. This was part of a big push to get the club going again. Meetings were now being held alternately in High Brooms and Langton. But sadly, the last recorded meeting was in Jan 1967.

Though I have no copies of issues 3, 4 & 7, I do have print run numbers for the first 5 editions.

No	Date	Print run	No of pages	Size of pages	Printing
1	Apr ‘56	25	4	Quarto	Typed + carbon copies
2	Apr ‘57	60	20	½ Quarto	Hand Duplicator
3	Dec ‘57	70	12	Quarto	Duplicated
4	Jul ‘58	86	12	Foolscap	Duplicated
5	Dec ‘58	99	12	Foolscap	Duplicated + stuck on photo
6	Jul ‘59	100?	16	Foolscap	Duplicated + stuck on photo
7	Dec ‘59		?	?	?
8	Jul ‘60	100	12	Foolscap	Duplicated with printed photo + adverts
9	Jan ‘61		16	½ foolscap	Duplicated with printed photo + adverts
10	Jul 61		16	Foolscap	Duplicated with printed photo + Adverts
11	Feb ‘62		8	Foolscap	Duplicated with printed photo + Adverts
12	Aug ‘62		8	Foolscap	Duplicated with printed photo + Adverts
13	Jan ‘63		4	Foolscap	Duplicated with printed photo + adverts
14	Jul ‘63	250	16	Foolscap	Duplicated with printed photo + adverts
15	Jan 64	?	8	Foolscap	Duplicated with printed photo + adverts
16	Aug ‘66	?	2	Foolscap	Duplicated

We always printed a few more than the membership as we sold a few at the Tunbridge Wells PS.

15) Competitions

One of the things suggested in the "How To Organise A Stamp Club" in " Stamp Finder" was have competitions.

I kept a book for recording all the competitions, but it seems I forgot to keep it up to date after 1958. But the rest were all recorded in the regular minutes. The booklet kept the quiz type records as well, but here I will mention only collection type competitions.

There seem to be 5 main types our members entered, plus once into Stampex. These were all competitions of showing one's collections, not quiz types, of which we held many as well.

1) **Our own competitions**

2a) Tunbridge Wells PS Junior competitions for The Melville

2b) Our entries into The Melville

2c) The Melville National

3) The Tunbridge Wells Hobbies Exhibitions.

1) Let us look at our own competitions first.

1st Competition at the 5th Meeting, May 16th 1953

Judge: Mr Hodgson (from 17 Newlands Rd) He also gave the prizes worth in total £1.

6 members entered

Winner John Teasdale

2nd Colin Fowle

3rd = David Lloyd-Roberts & Myself

2nd Competition at the 9th meeting, Oct 3rd 1953

Judges: Humphrey Smeeton & Bobby Ely

8 members entered

Winner Robert Holland

2nd Myself, 3rd John Teasdale

3rd Competition at the 23rd meeting, Jan 9th 1954

Judges: Humphrey Smeeton, Bobby Ely & M. Ellis

5 entries

Winner Myself

2nd Robert Holland, 3rd John Teasdale.

4th Competition at the 40th Meeting, 9th May 1954

Judges: Bobby Ely, Humphrey Smeeton, Myself, and Mrs Jenkins (Non-collector - we asked a non-collector to help judge)

7 members entered

Winner Virginia & Simon Timmis (Joint entry)

2nd Colin Fowle, 3rd John Teasdale

5th Competition at 50th Meeting, Dec 17th 1955

Judges: Bobby Ely, Myself & Mrs Jenkins.

Presented by The Mayoress of Tunbridge Wells.

10 members entered

Winner Virginia Timmis

2nd Peter Powell, 3rd Simon Timmis

6th Competition at the 70th Meeting, Oct 13 1956

Judges: Messrs Cartwright, Brewer, Williams, Yardley & Miss Brett

Presented by His Worship The Mayor (Councillor Muffet)

Class A. 11 members entered.

Winner Patrick Hoyte

2nd Colin Fowle, 3rd David Reich

Class B. 5 members entered

Winner Peter Lewis

2nd Bronwyn Lloyd-Roberts, 3rd Susan Smith

7th Competition at the 100th meeting, Sept 28th 1957

Judges: Messrs Cartwright, Read & Williams

Presented by Wilfrid B Haworth MA, Editor of "Stamp Collectors' Fortnightly"

TROPHY "Newlands Stamp" (Silver stamp on shield)

Class A (10 Members entered out of 11 eligible)

Winner David Reich & Patrick Hoyte

3rd Colin Fowle

Class B (9 members entered out of 11 eligible)

Winner Christopher Bayly

2nd Peter Powell, 3rd Bronwen Phillips

The annual Trophy that used to be awarded in the annual competitions of the Newlands Road Philatelic Society. It was called the Newlands Stamp. My father carved the oak wood shield, and the silver parts were attached and engraved by L. Reich & Sons from Monson Road.

The shield now has its silver stamp removed because it was gifted to the Melville Memorial national Stamp competition for juniors in 1979 - and was first awarded to the Boston School Stamp Club that I ran when I was teaching there, at the London 1980 International Stamp Exhibition.

Five years later it was awarded to the next school where I was a teacher and had formed another successful stamp club, Claremont Fan Court School, of Esher, London, in Autumn 1985.

STAMP BUG NEWS

No 9 JULY 1981

SCHOOL STAMP CLUB FOCUS

Boston Grammar School's stamp society houses a thriving stamp business

FIRST day covers mean more to the members of Boston Grammar School's stamp club than to most people — they design their own.

Every time the Post Office issues a special set of stamps the club produces and sells its own covers complete with special design and handstamp.

It's just one of the many activities undertaken by the members of the club who last year won two individual prizes and the Schools' Trophy at the Melville Awards. (You will read later that the Schools' Trophy has a very special meaning to the club).

The club's leader is maths teacher Mr Chris Phillips, the man behind the school's first day cover service. He believes in making meetings as varied and interesting as possible and uses a variety of methods to do so.

His club meets twice a week — on Tuesday lunchtimes and evenings — and activities include talks by guest speakers from clubs outside the school, auctions and, once a year, their own version of philatelic Mastermnind.

Involved

Said Mr Phillips: "We have 30 members and I like them all to become involved with the club as much as possible. We even have our own officers, a chairman, a secretary, a treasurer and an auctioneer.

Because of our first day cover service and auctions we are completely self financing and in the two and a half years the club has been running we've been able to buy an ultra violet lamp, a watermark detector, mount cutters and a variety of philatelic books. I think we were also one of the first school clubs to become Stamp Bug members."

The school's first day cover service has been in operation since the club was formed. Mr Phillips's connection with covers, however, goes back to the 1950s — as does his connection with running stamp clubs.

He takes up the story: "It all began in 1952 when I lived in Tunbridge Wells, Kent. Three boys asked me to organise a street stamp club in the town's Newlands Road."

The club went from strength to strength and in 1957 it started its first day cover service with the World Scout Jubilee Jamboree issue.

With the profits made from the sale of the covers the club had the "Newlands Stamp" made and members competed for it each year in a competition.

Inevitably, the club disbanded as its members grew older and left the area. Mr Phillips was left with the Newlands Stamp.

Continued Mr Phillips: "I didn't really know what to do with the stamp so two years ago I offered it to the Melville Committee along with £20 to use as an extra prize.

"They accepted it and had the silver stamp remounted on a wooden block. The stamp became the School's Trophy and you can imagine my pleasure when we became its first winner."

One of the club's individual Melville winners was 16-year-old Tim Sylvester, a keen member. He's been collecting for the past eight years and has built his collection on British and Canadian stamps.

Collections

Said Tim: "I collect mainly Canadian stamps because my mother and grandmother both collect British issues. It seemed pointless the three of us having the same stamps. I hope one day they'll pass their collections on to me."

Tim has also tried his hand at designing some of the club's first day covers but pride of place for this goes to another 16 year old, Simon Meeds.

Simon has designed five covers for the club including the recent Folklore and Liverpool and Manchester Railway issues. His latest achievement has been the club's design for last month's National Trust set.

Said Mr Phillips: "We have some really fine artists amongst us and we are all very proud of our service."

The club's next first day cover is, of course, for the Royal Wedding issue. As you might expect it's an extremely effective design.

Stamp Bug News was published once a month by the Post Office.

8th Competition at the 135th meeting, Sept 27th 1958

Judges: (Probably Mr Cartwright & Miss Brett + other)
Presented by Kenneth F Chapman, Editor of
"Stamp Collecting Weekly"
"Newlands Stamp" Winner - Peter Powell
Class A Winners Christopher Phillips & Patrick Hoyte
3rd David Beeby

Class B Winner Peter Powell
2nd David Taylor, 3rd Bronwen Phillips

Best New Member - Simon Levett
Good try by youngest member - Margaret Collier

9th Competition at the 166th meeting, Sept 26th 1959

Judges: (Probably Mr Cartwright & Miss Brett + other)
Presented by James Watson
(Assist Editor "Gibbons Stamp Monthly".
"Newlands Stamp" winner - Christopher Selmes
Class A Winner Christopher Selmes
2nd Patrick Hoyte 3rd Christopher Phillips

Class B winner Bronwen Phillips
2nd Patrick Smith, 3rd Susan Smith
Thematic Prize Simon Levett
Best new member John Symon

10th competition at the 200th meeting, 22nd Oct 1960

Presented by Charles P Rang, Editor of
"Gibbons Stamp Monthly"
"Newlands Stamp" winner - Simon Levett
Class A Winner Simon Levett
2nd Christopher Selmes, 3rd= Susan Smith & Peter Powell

Class B Winner Bronwen Phillips
2nd Patrick Smith; 3rd Bronwyn Lloyd-Roberts
Best New Member Angela Penn

11th Competition at the 226th meeting, November 18th 1961

Presented by Cyril Harmer, of Harmers Auctions
"Newlands Stamp" - Patrick Smith
Class A Winner Peter Powell
2nd Patrick Hoyte, 3rd Susan Smith
Class B Winner Patrick Smith
2nd Margaret Collier 3rd Derek Camfield
Best New Member Graham Camfield

12th Competition at the 242nd Meeting, 6th October 1962

Presented by Mr Brown, Stamp Designer of Harrison & Sons (UK & World) Printers of postage Stamps.
"Newlands Stamp" Patrick Smith & Peter Powell
Class A Winner Peter Powell
2nd Susan Smith, 3rd David Green.
Class B Winner Patrick Smith
2nd Derek Camfield, 3rd Tony Matthews
Best New Member Michael Grenville

13th Competition at the 263rd Meeting, October 19th 1963

Judges: Mr J C Cartwright & Mr D Read
Presented by Mr Toms MBE. (Writer of a Paper in last year's Philatelic Congress of GB Book, about Junior clubs)
"Newlands Stamp" - Peter Powell
Class A Winner Peter Powell
2nd Shirley Burr 3rd Bronwen Phillips
Class B Winner Graham Camfield
2nd Tad Stone 3rd Mark Nicholson

14th Competition at the 283rd Meeting, Nov 21 1964

Presented by Mr Pearce (Tunbridge Wells PS)
Winner Mark Nicholson (Name should be on Newlands Stamp but it isn't)
2nd David Green, 3rd Graham Camfield

This was the last of the annual collection competitions.

The Melville Memorial National Junior Competition was organised in memory of Fred J Melville, who was a KEEN supporter of young collectors, by the Philatelic Congress of Great Britain. Anyone under 17 from anywhere in the WORLD could enter, but entries had to be submitted by a member society. So our members' entries were at first put into the Tunbridge Wells PS annual Junior competition, and were thus competing with children from schools in the neighbourhood. Later, when our society became a member of The PC of GB in 1959, we were able to enter our own members through our own society as well as the TWPS!

There were 3 classes: A) Between 15 & under 17, B) 12 & under 15 & C) Under 12s, & later a D) class for 17 to 21s.

2a) Tunbridge Wells PS Junior competitions for Melville

1954. Only I myself entered when I came 1st in Class B. I won a Certificate Of Merit, collected at the Brighton PC of GB meeting.

1955 Class A 2nd Myself
Class B 2nd John Teasdale
(Only winners could be sent for national judging).

1956 Class A 2nd Myself
Class B 3rd Patrick Hoyte
Class C *1st Peter Powell Won Cert Of Merit In National*
2nd Susan Smith

1957 Class A 6th was Colin Fowle
Class B 3rd was David Reich
Class C 1st Peter Powell + Melville Cert of Merit
(11 MEMBERS ENTERED THAT YEAR.)

1958 18 members entered in 1958
Class A 3rd Simon Levett
Class B *1st Patrick Hoyte + Melville Certif of Merit*
2nd Peter Powell + Melville Certif of Merit
Class C 1st Bronwen Phillips + Melville of Certif of Merit

1959 At least 9 members entered

Class A 2nd Simon Levett
3rd Patrick Hoyte
Class B *1st Christopher Selmes + Melville Cert of Merit*
Highly Commended Peter Powell
Class C *1st Bronwen Phillips + Melville Certif of Merit*
2nd Roger Smith

1960 New class D added (Ages 17 - 21)

Class D *1st Christopher Phillips*
Class A *2nd Christopher Selmes* ***3rd in actual Melville***
3rd Patrick Hoyte
Class B *2nd Susan Smith*
3rd Peter Powell Certif of Merit

And 2b) (Our own judging of those not sent up by TWPS)

Class D 1st Simon Levett
Class A 1st Christopher Selmes (3rd in actual Melville)
2nd Patrick Hoyte; 3rd David Reich
Class B *1st Bronwen Phillips*
2nd Bronwyn Lloyd Roberts
3rd Phyllchen Herrick
Class C *1st Patrick Smith*

AND 2c) THE MELVILLE

Class A 3rd (H/C) Christopher Selmes (On display at the Royal Festival Hall, London, International Exhibition)
Class B Certif of Merit Peter Powell.
1960 was our best year ever.

1961 **2a)** Class A 2nd Peter Powell
Class B *1st Susan Smith*
Class C 2nd Patrick Smith
2b) Class A *1st Peter Powell*
Class B *1st Bronwen Phillips*
Class C *1st Patrick Smith*

Sadly no one won any awards in the actual Melville this year.

1962 **2a**) Class C 2nd Graham Camfield
3rd Graham Edwards

2b) Class A *1st Peter Powell*
Class B *1st Bronwen Phillips*
2nd Shirley Burr
Class C *1st Graham Camfield*
2c) No winners in Melville.

1963 **2b)** Class A *1st Peter Powell*
Class B *1st Bronwen Phillips*
Class C *1st Michael Leiblin*
2nd David Green
3rd Roger Bradgate

1964 **2b)** Class 16 - 20 *1st Shirley Burr*
2nd Bronwen Phillips,
3rd Peter Powell
Class 13 - 15 *1st Graham Camfield*
2nd Mark Nicholson
Class under 13 *1st Graham Edwards*

3) Tunbridge Wells Hobbies Exhibition
April 1956.
3rd in the Open Christopher Phillips 15/- prize.
April 1957
15 members entered
2nd Prize David Reich (5/-)
H/C Christopher Bayly & Patrick Hoyte
April 1958
I seem to have lost all that year's records in this contest.
April 1959
Junior Class 1st Christopher Selmes Cup & 15/-
Senior Class H/C Christopher Phillips
April 1960

Junior 1st Christopher Selmes Cup & 10/-
2nd Bronwen Phillips
3rd Peter Powell
H/C Susan Smith & Ivan Trussler
Open H/C David Reich
Thematic 2nd Patrick Hoyte

1961

Juniors 3rd Caroline Collier
Open 2nd Christopher Phillips

1962

Juniors H/C Patrick Smith
Open 2nd Christopher Phillips
The Hobbies exhibition ceased about now I think.

Members also took part in other occasional competitions outside of the normal club events:

Wilfrid B Haworth contest
Kent Federation

Our membership cards looked like this:-

NEWLANDS ROAD PHILATELIC SOCIETY
(Founded 15 April 1953)

MEMBERSHIP CARD

Name CHRISTOPHER PHILLIPS

No. 3 Peter Powell
Secretary

Christopher Phillips
President

16) What did we do in Meetings?

Obviously no club can survive for long on just having competitions, speakers and a newsletter.

The club was run by a committee of annually elected members. The usual officers were the President (originally called the "chief"), the Secretary, the Treasurer, an Auctioneer, Editor, and often Assistants to each of these. All committee members were under 21.

Past Presidents were Robin Grey (1953-54) John Teasdale (1954-55) Colin Fowle (1955-59) Christopher Phillips (1959-60) Patrick Hoyte (1960-62) Peter Powell (1962-65) David Green (1965–66) Robert Romer (1966-67)

Past Secretaries Christopher Phillips (1953–59) Peter Powell (1959-62) Shirley Burr (1962-64) Lynda Bringloe (1962–66) Andrew Crighton (1966-7).

One of the most regular meetings was an auction sale, which helped raise money for the club funds. Often we had members giving short displays.

We also had the occasional treasure hunt, swopping meetings. Other popular meetings consisted of philatelic versions of well know radio type games. Some of the games we played at meetings were:

Just a Minute (Try to speak for one minute without hesitation, repetition or deviation on a stamp subject)
Twenty Questions (Members try to guess the Philatelic term, expression, etc the member is thinking of, by asking up to 20 questions, only Y or N answers)
"What's My Stamp" Similar to 20 Questions but a particular well known stamp.
"Brain of NRPS" (Similar to Brain of Britain)

A couple of times, we were invited to display at

the Tunbridge Wells PS.

We had visits to printing works in Tonbridge (Whitefriars) and the Kent & Sussex Courier. We were also shown round the Tunbridge Wells Post Office Sorting Office.

For three new years running we had meetings in London! Yes, that meant getting up early (around 4.30 am) to catch the first trains.

The first such visit (January 1957) was to see "Stamp Collecting Weekly" being printed. We started off in the Offices in Maiden Lane, and met the Editor (Kenneth Chapman) and his assistant (O.W. Newport). After they told us about how the editorial side was conducted, we were taken to the printing works, where the Printing Manager showed us round. Everyone left with a FREE copy of that week's issue. Then, after browsing in some Strand Stamp shops (and a little purchasing!) we went to the British Museum and saw the stamp collections they had. Sandwiches in Trafalgar Square were eaten amongst the lions & pigeons! Then we made a visit to the News Cinema before travelling home by train.

The following year, just two of us went to see the De La Rue Exhibition in Regent Street, and saw a film and talk about stamp printing. We each got some free De La Rue sample stamps.

In January 1959 we met for the first time our postal member, David Keating (Edgeware), in London to be shown round Stanley Gibbons, and see how they do their regular business. We saw the New Issue Dept and the Rare Stamps Dept. David Keating actually wrote the article about this in the July 1959 edition of Newlands Post. I would like to say Gibbons gave us a Penny Black each, but sadly we had to be content with just SEEING very rare stamps. We ate our sandwiches in Trafalgar Square under the watchful right eye of Lord Nelson on high. Foyled again, methinks, because that is where we next went: Foyles Bookshop (which had a stamp department). To round off the day we saw three films in the De La Rue offices in Regent Street, one about stamp printing and the others about playing cards!

In 1960, it was the London International Stamp Exhibition at The Royal Festival Hall, July 9th-16th.

I was one of the lucky ones to be an official steward throughout the show. The Philatelic Congress was also held here for three of those days, and I attended some of those meetings as well. By now I was too old to be a member of the club I had started 7 years previously, but I had become an Honorary member, along with the other two founders. One of the members, Christopher Selmes, was honoured by having his Melville entry on display (he had come third in his year group). So it was quite natural for the NRPS members to come up here for a day's visit. Not only did they see Christopher's exhibit, but also those of the other prize winners.

The whole exhibition was estimated to have been worth £10 Million (a heck of a lot in 1960). One of the most unusual exhibits was a violin made entirely from (about 12,000) stamps (except for the strings!) There was an amusing tannoy announcement: "Attention Please, Attention Please, will the small boy who bought a set of Malaysian stamps at stand No. 3 for 2/5½ please collect his change from a one pound note. I will repeat that...". Another announcement was directly aimed at our own club group: "Will Caroline Collier of the Newlands Road Stamp Club please report to the main entrance, where her sister Margaret is waiting for her." So FAME AT LAST IN LONDON!

Kent & Sussex Courier 25th Oct 1963

PRESIDENT MAKES IT THREE

MR. ALFRED TOMS, of Christchurch, Hampshire, presented the prizes for the annual stamp competition held by the Newlands Road Philatelic Society of Tunbridge Wells, at Culverden House on Saturday. The Newlands Stamp Shield was won for the third time by the society's president, Peter Powell.

Mr. Toms spoke about the society at last year's Philatelic Congress of Great Britain as the only self-run junior society he knew, and on Saturday he talked to members about his collection.

Prize winners were: Newlands Stamp sheld, Peter Powell; seniors, 1 Peter Powell, 2 Shirley Burr, 3 Bronwen Phillips, 4 David Green; juniors, 1 Graham Camfield, 2 Tad Stone, 3 Mark Nicholson, 4 Michael Grenville; consolation, Lynda Bringloe, Michael Leibling, Derek Camfield, Graham Edwards.

The judges were Mr. J. C. Cartwright, an honorary member and Mr. D. Read, a Tunbridge Wells stamp dealer.

FIRST DAY COVER
1st Aug. 1957
1857~1957
B. P.
DIAMOND
JUBILEE
JAMBOREE
JUBILEE JAMBOREE
Christopher
(Hon. Sec.& Treas. N.R.P.S)
15, Newlands Road,
TUNBRIDGE WELLS,
Kent.

BY AIR MAIL
1st. Day
Cover.
Christopher Phillips,
(Hon Sec. & Treas. of the NR PS.)
15, Newlads Road,
TUNBRIDGE WELLS,
Kent.

NEW DEFINITIVE
1892 ~ 2 6 3 lbs.
1958 ~ 1 lb 2 ozs.
FIRST DAY COVER
Christopher Phillips
c/o 87, Berengrave Lane.
RAINHAM,
Nr. Gillingham.
Kent.

BRITISH EMPIRE
GAMES
CARDIFF
1958
JULY 18TH — 26TH
FIRST DAY COVER
Issued by the Newlands Road
Philatelic Society
Designed by Patrick Hoyte
NEWLANDS ROAD PHILATELIC
SOCIETY,
Tunbridge Wells,
Kent

17) First Day Covers

All clubs need some way of financing them to run. For the first 4 years the club relied upon subscriptions and auction sale commissions to keep it going, as well as donations. Money was needed for Library books, prizes and the Newsletter.

Then in 1957, the Post Office did something VERY unusual. It decided to issue a set of three special stamps to celebrate the Jubilee Scout Jamboree, that year being held in Sutton Coldfield.

This was so unusual, because the last time a new set of stamps had been issued was for the Coronation, a set of 4, in 1953.

A friend had given us a hand-held duplicator, and we used this to print our own First Day Covers. The design was by Norman Timmis, the Art master at The Skinners' School. We sold the envelopes separately at 4d each (Members only,1d). But we sold the complete set on the cover posted on the first day for 2/4.

THEN we found that there was to be a special cancellation at the Jubilee Jamboree in Sutton Coldfield.

As I had an Aunt living near there, I decided to cycle all the way from Tunbridge Wells to Sutton Coldfield to post our covers there. It was only about 200 miles. I spent two days cycling to my Aunt's, and on the third day I cycled to the camp site in Sutton Coldfield, in time to buy the new stamps, on the first day of issue (Aug 1st), stick the stamps on the addressed covers and post them in the special post box at the mobile Post Office on the site. As far as we know, all the 80 or so covers I posted arrived at the correct addresses and all for 2/4! These actual covers have been seen selling for £40 or more in Auction. So all those people who invested 2 shillings and 4 old pence (about 12p!) are now rich!

Well, that was one way to keep fit! After staying a few days with my aunt, I returned home by cycling the 200 miles back in two more days. So you see collecting stamps keeps you fit! (Philately gets you everywhere!)

Not content with having one new issue after 4 years of none, they decided in their wisdom to issue another! But it was hardly noticed by anyone because it was a slightly altered ordinary 4d stamp to celebrate the 46th Parliamentary Conference in London that year on the 12th Sept. They also issued a special airletter. I decided to walk to do this FDC service, as we posted them in our local Post Office in St Johns Road, and only about 12 covers were done. So this is very rare!

After that we needed a good rest from new Issues, but the Post Office decided that it quite liked making loads of money and decided on another stamp celebration. This time, in July 1958, the British Empire Games were being held in Wales, and the Post Office went mad and issued three more new stamps with a slightly higher face value of 2/- .

Now this is where we struck lucky.

First of all, Charles Lusted had our covers printed professionally, 1000 this time (instead of the 100 of the Scouts issue). The design was based on one by Patrick Hoyte, improved by Mr Lusted for printing. We decided to sell these for 4d each envelope, plus 5d for servicing and posting in Cardiff, plus an extra 2d if a card stiffener was included. Now how to sell so many? We put in adverts in Stamp Collecting Weekly and Philatelic Magazine. Gibbons Monthly at that time did not have any advertising, but the editors gave us a

WONDERFUL free article about our covers, and the day after publication, orders started pouring in by post; several arrived at both daily deliveries. We were getting sales for the envelopes as well as fully serviced covers.

The other GOOD news was that the Headmaster of The Skinners' School allowed me to have the day off school to go to Cardiff to post the covers. So on the 18th July 1958, I went by train from Tunbridge Wells to Cardiff, via Charing Cross & Paddington, and back in the one day.

I planned in advance, and wrote a letter to the Trafalgar Square Post Office asking them to have ready a certain amount of stamps for well over 300 covers. I had a letter back saying they could not do that. So imagine my surprise that, when I arrived at opening time and asked for over 300 sets, they told me that they had them all ready for me! The trouble was I had had a few extra orders since, so they had to count out a few more sets. But I got all I needed and proceeded by tube to Paddington Station, bearing all my stamps and covers. (I did not know about marmalade sandwiches under hats at that time).

I boarded my train and found a seat with a table, and started sticking on the 3d stamps, much to the surprise of other passengers. Several pairs of eyes glued themselves on to me. I got asked things like "Where on earth did you get all those stamps?".... "You certainly have a LOT of friends!"...."Did you pay for all those stamps?"...."Are you a millionaire?" It was bad enough trying to stick the stamps on straight & symmetrical on a wobbly train, without being distracted by these questions... By the time I had reached Cardiff, I had not even put on all the 3d stamps. Luckily, the main Post Office was only a short distance from the station. I found a seat and table and spent the rest of the day and afternoon sticking on the rest of the stamps. Even then I was interrupted, but this time they wanted to BUY some of the few blank covers that I had left to sell; I sold about 36 that way! More profit for the club! Finally, just in time, I finished sticking on all the stamps, and posted the 300+ covers in the special Post Box to obtain the special postmark, and only had a few minutes spare to catch the last train back home!

One cover somehow managed to have been posted without a single stamp on! And about 4 customers complained that the Post office had damaged one or more of the stamps. All these were compensated from the 12 or so spare FDC we sent to ourselves to sell on afterwards. Altogether it was the best fund raiser we ever did. About £15 was raised for the club funds, thanks mainly to Stanley Gibbons' free write-up.

Then as in the previous year, another, but strange new announcement came from the Post Office. On the 8th of August the Post office announced Regional stamps to be issued, for sale only in each of the 6 regions, Scotland, Wales, Northern Ireland, Isle Of Man, Jersey & Guernsey: a 3d stamp for each, and for the 3 large regions, at a later date, 6d & 1/3 stamps. This threw us into confusion, for we could not visit all 6 regions on the day issue. My bicycle was not fast

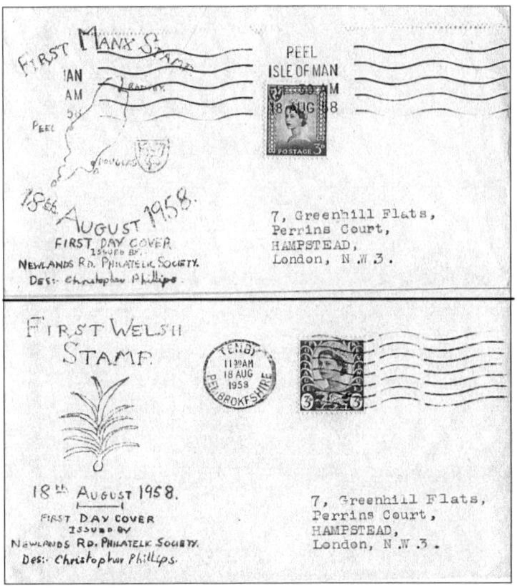

enough!

My Uncle lived in IOM and he did that FDC for us, and one member (David Beeby) was going on holiday to Wales and did that one. So we missed out on the other regions, and the two higher values.

The next issue was not a Commemorative, but just a new value of a definitive, a 4½d. The last and only time a 4½d stamp had been issued was in 1892! So we did a FDC for this issue. (The design of the cover was based on the Victorian stamp.)

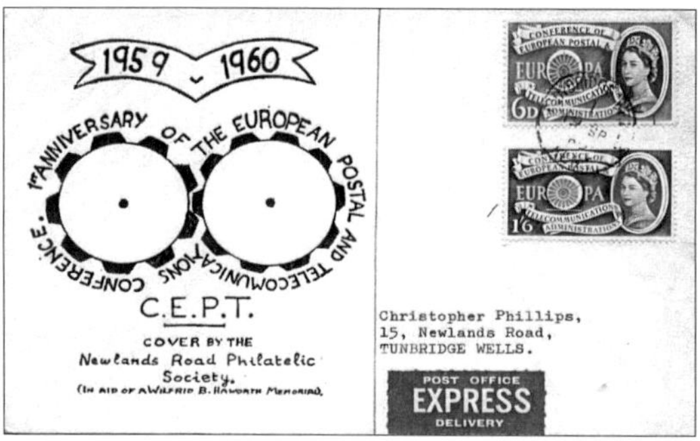

There were two commemorative sets issued in 1960. There was a special cancellation in Eastbourne, so I cycled to Eastbourne and back for the day to post those covers. I see covers with this postmark now sell for £125!

Two months later there was a pair of stamps for C.E.P.T. For this issue we had our covers professionally printed, instead of using the hand-held duplicator, and tried to raise money for the Wilfrid B Haworth Memorial fund, but sadly we hardly made any profit, as we had too many printed.

In 1961, the Post Office went really mad and had three special issues! Firstly for the Centenary of the Post Office Savings Bank, next a set for the 2nd conference of Europa, and finally for the Commonwealth Parliamentary Conference. Sadly for me, I lost my only copy I had of the Europa Cover, and had to buy someone else's. None of our covers for these special issues was posted in a town where there was a special cancellation, although the bought in one is the Torquay one and is more valuable.

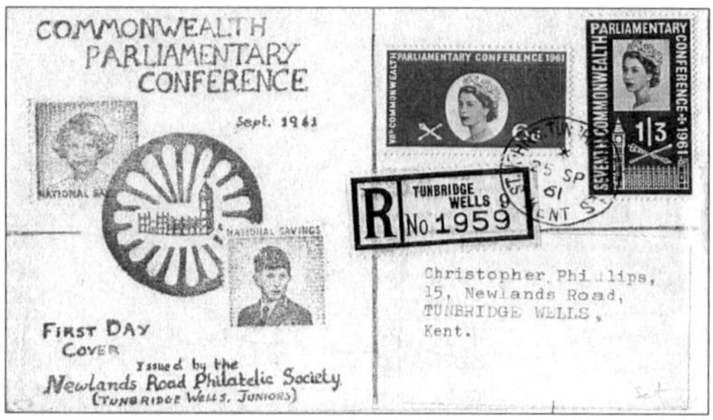

The following year, 1962, the Post Office must have needed a rest! They had only ONE new set, but they were experimenting with new sorting machinery during that year. After the disappointing trials with graphite lines on the backs of the stamps, to aid sorting letters into 1st & 2nd class mail automatically, they came up with another innovation, which obviously worked, because now all stamps have the Phosphor bars overprinted on them. The 1962 issue for National Productivity Year was the first time commemorative stamps were treated in this way, but sadly for me, those Phosphor stamps were on sale only in the Southampton Post Office region. So we were unable to do a service for those, just the ordinary stamps.

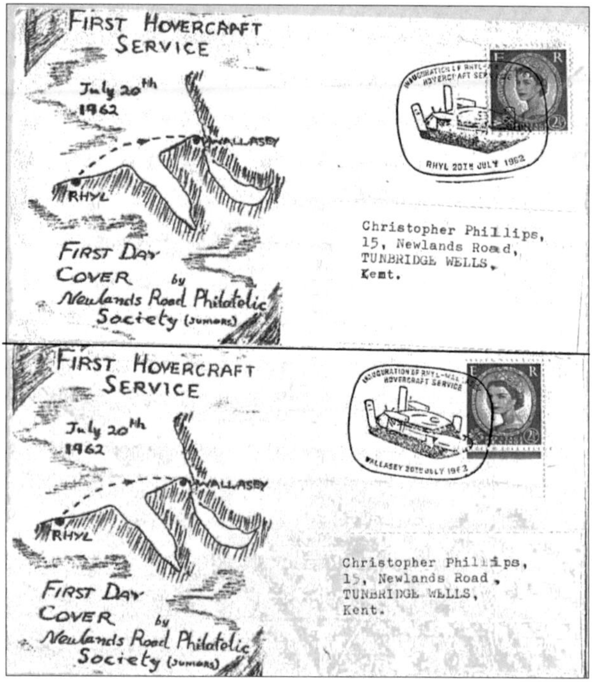

Also in 1962, there was a special cancellation for the first Hovercraft service between Rhyll and Wallasey. There were no special stamps, but we did run a FDC service for this. We posted our 20 or so covers to both ends in advance and back came our covers, nicely postmarked.

Then in 1963 it was a REALLY BIG YEAR for new stamps and our club.

At this stage I was at the Medway College Of Technology, and one of my fellow students had an

Adana Printing Press, and he printed our First Day Covers for 1962 & 1963. We used the same basic design (map of The British Isles), changing just the headings. In 1963 the Post Office really stepped up their money making ideas. There were 6 special issues.

All had the Ordinary & Phosphor varieties, so that meant 12 FDC to be serviced. Additionally, our club was now 10 years old, and for the day of our Exhibition (see chapter 22 for the full story) we had a special cover printed, slightly altering the one we did for the Empire Games back in 1958. All these covers can be seen in full colour on one page. (I have not displayed the Phosphor covers as they look the same, but they are much more valuable.)

The next step forward was that I bought my own Adana printing machine in 1964, and from then on I printed all our own FDCs. We found a block maker, so from our own designs we printed all our own FDCs. The first such cover was for the Shakespeare Festival. The printing was not as good quality as I would have liked, but future covers came out better. To acquire the Phosphor stamps I needed, I had to travel up to London, and buy them at the London Bridge Post Office, having bought the ordinary stamps in Tunbridge Wells St Johns Road PO. This added to the cost of production, but we still made a profit, even after taking off the cost of the day return to London. By now we were building up a regular list of clients, many of whom paid for a year in advance for all their FDCs; several had BOTH covers but many (sadly for them) did not take up the Phosphor varieties. All the covers were now in two or three colours, which meant the covers had to be printed three times, one for each colour. One thing I had to learn straight away was to make a mould for the envelope to fit (Continued on page 103)

6 in 1963

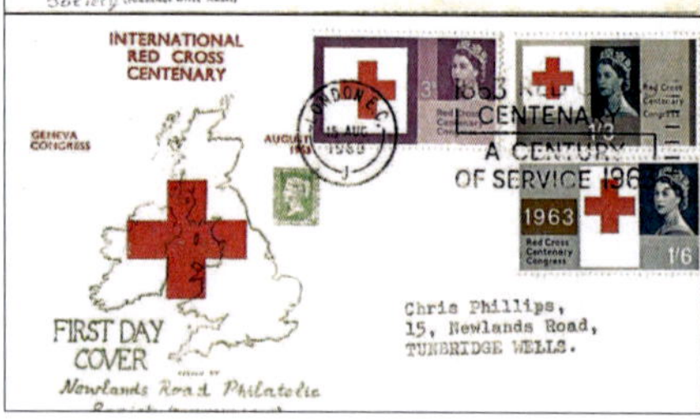

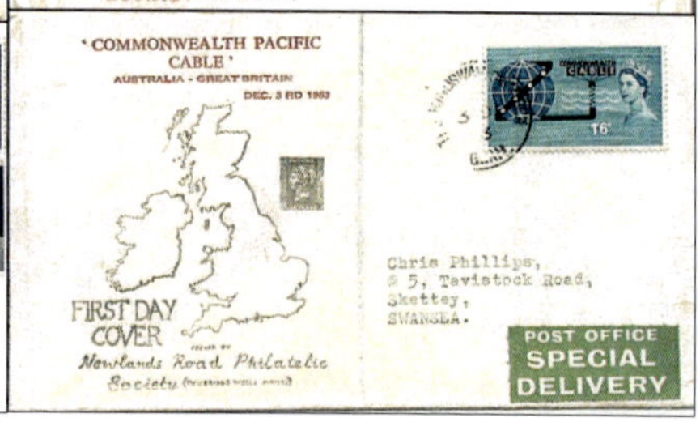

The purple cancel is not an actual Postmark, just a self produced cachet

in, so that there was a an even flat surface to print on, due to the different thicknesses where the envelope was stuck on the back. So I needed two such moulds for the two most common sizes of envelopes we used.

(Continued on page 107)

4 in 1964

9 in 1965

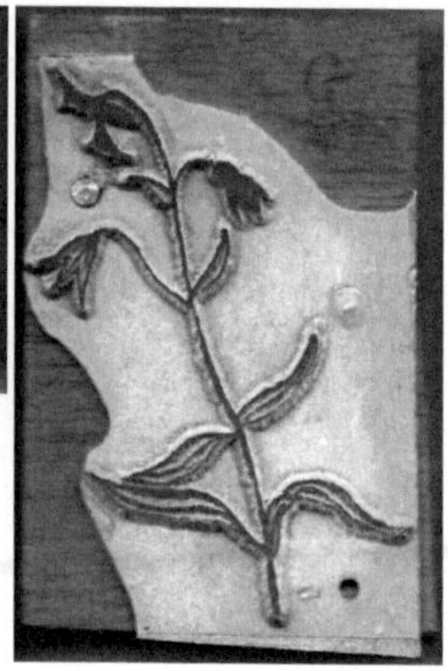

These are the 5 printing blocks used, along with typeface, to print the Botanical Congress covers. 4 colours were used in all, red, blue, green & black (typeface). Each printing had to be exactly in the right place. Those covers went through 4 separate printings.

Three colours were used for the Geographical covers: two for the design (red & blue) and black for the typeface.

Same for the Shakespeare covers

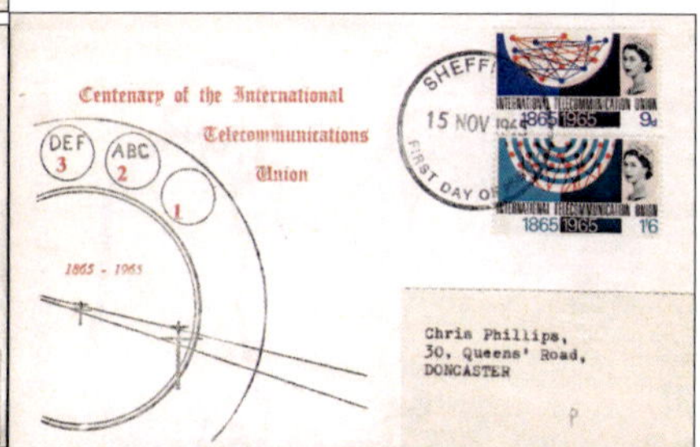

8 in 1966

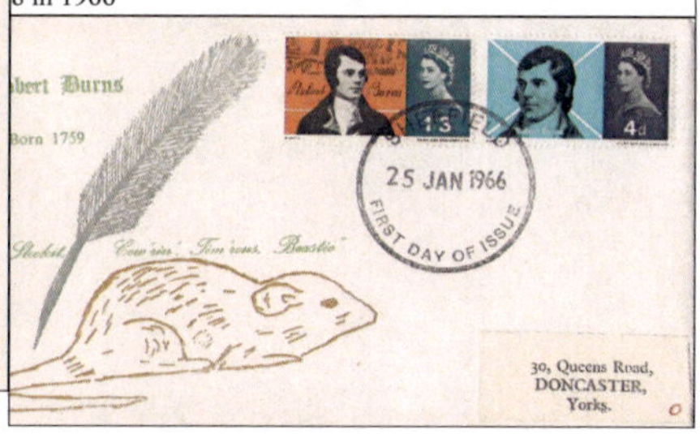

The printing blocks for the Post Office Tower. The Map was used many times for various covers.

I had the blocks made for a whole year in advance, so we

paid for only ONE block, and I cut up the block into the separate parts. This saved a lot of money. The blocks were either pinned or later stuck on a wooden block with double-sided sticky tape.

In some later pictures I am showing a few of the printing blocks we had made to print the cover's picture parts of the design. I am showing in reduced sizes all the FDCs that were produced to raise money for the NRPS. In 1963/64 I was at Swansea University for a year on a teacher training course. In Sept 1964 I started teaching at Edlington Comprehensive School, near Doncaster. It was not long before I had started a school stamp club there. Obviously I was no longer able to attend NRPS meetings, and I decided to divide the profits from the FDCs equally between the NRPS and the School Club. After the first year there, some pupils started designing the covers and others buying them. This situation continued until Jan 1967, when the NRPS held its last meeting. But I did not know this, and continued for some time saving profits equally. I sold the cover now under a registered business name "PHILCOVERS". The NRPS money continued to build up and over £100 was in the "kitty" by the time I found out the NRPS had in effect closed down. I continued to produce FDCs for many more years, and the profits from the covers were shared equally between the past and present School stamp club as I moved from one school to another. I finished printing my own FDCs at Xmas 1983, but carried on for a couple more years selling Cotswold FDC's instead. (Also Official Post Office covers.)

What the printing blocks looked like

18) Tunbridge Wells Hobbies Exhibition

In 1958 we first had a non-competitive stand at this well-run exhibition. Prior to this year, a few members had been entering in the Philatelic competitive exhibits, and winning certificates. We noticed that other clubs had stands, and so we asked if we could have one too. So in 1958 the only all junior stamp club had its own stall at the regular annual Tunbridge Wells Hobbies Exhibition. For our first year we had the stall outside the main entrance, but where everyone had to pass to get in. We thought it would be a good way to get new members. It was open for 5 days, in the Easter School Holidays. Many members took it in turns to be present at the exhibition to keep the displays safe. The stamps and covers were the properties of several members.

In 1959 we repeated our efforts, and widely publicised our stand with Posters and mentions in the National Philatelic Press, and we got much more interest.

This time we had added attractions, rather than just a static display. Malcolm Clift had made an electrical Quiz, in which, when the correct answer was given, the light lit! Members whose stamps were on display included Chris Phillips, Patrick Hoyte, Peter Powell, Peter Veness, Christina Hindle, David Reich and Phyllchen Herrick. Some of our library books and watermark detectors were also on display. One of the attractions, though, was the special competition, in which we had put 25 questions, one on each of the other stands. Only non-members could take part. 20

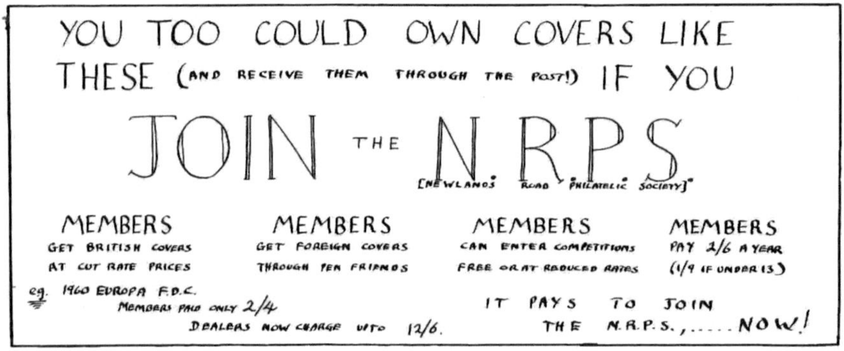

1959

boys and girls entered; the two winners got a prize which include a FREE membership of the club for the next year. The winner was David Harding, aged 12, with 90%. John Symon, aged 14, was 2nd with 88%.

We also had a voting form for people to vote for their favourite Regional stamp. 80 people voted, 20 of whom were members.

The clear winner was Scotland 1/3 (34 votes),
2nd Guernsey 3d (15 votes).

Not content with all this activity, we also had a petition to the Post Office, asking for small pictorial postage stamps. Over 100 people signed it. Two weeks later, the PO spokesman was rather negative in his response.

For 1960 we were awarded a Trade stand cubicle for our display. (See the picture on next page)

As in 1959, we had displays by members (Christopher Phillips, Patrick Hoyte, and Peter Powell). In the thematic display we had a philatelic Royal Tree and in part this was helped by Stanley Gibbons giving us a free copy of a book (Stamp Portraits of the Queen). Last year's "PhilyQuiz" was again very popular. Under 16, non-members could also enter a free

guess the number of stamps in the jar. B Tomlinson was the winner with a guess of 587. He was the nearest to 586, and he won the jar of stamps.

We had a poll of visitors to see if they'd prefer to have small pictorial stamps, instead of just the Queen and the squiggles. 332 voted in favour and only 27 against, and 335 signed the petition. But still the Postmaster General said there was no "demand". (Full details of this campaign are in its own chapter).

Again in 1961 we were lucky to have the use of a trade like stand, right near the entrance, giving us a little extra room for displays. Displays were by Susan and Patrick Smith, Patrick Hoyte, Bronwen Phillips, David Beeby, Angela Penn, Shirley Burr, Peter Powell and Margaret Collier. The main title was made entirely from old, cheap stamps. The colours were chosen

to give a rainbow effect (idea by Margaret Collier). Susan Smith was praised heartily for all the hard work she did to help look after and helping erecting, displaying and stewarding, as well as dismantling. Malcolm Clift's "PhilyQuiz" was back with much use by the visitors. Again there was a Guess the Number of Stamps in a Jar competition. About 250 children had a go. The main theme of the display was Land, Sea & Air (+ Space).

The last time we took part was in 1962. I am not sure if this was also the last Hobbies exhibition or not. But I do not remember hearing about any more after 1962. We were lucky to have the same good position as 1961, and this year's theme was "Today's Menu". Much of this display was by Susan & Patrick Smith. Malcolm Clift's ever popular "PhilyQuiz" was the usual success. Instead of guessing the number of stamps in a Jar, we had Guess the Number of Stamp

Magazines in a box! That was won by Michael Grenville of Hildenborough. Visitors were asked to judge the best stamp of 1961. The winner was the Swiss Pro Juventute 10 + 10 Cents. The winning Commonwealth stamp was the Ghana £1.

Another fact we found out from a poll was that 80% of stamp collectors do not belong to any stamp club!

Susan Smith looking after the stand.

NEWLANDS ROAD PHILATELIC SOCIETY

THIS is an all-junior society founded on April 15th, 1953. Membership is open to all young people between the ages of ten and twenty years, the subscription being 1/9 or 2/6 according to age. We have twenty meetings a year which include: auction sales, talks by well-known philatelists, visits to printing works as well as an annual party and at least one visit to London. The "Newlands Post" is issued twice a year and is free to all members. We have a good selection of books in the library, some of which you can see here.

Our stand this year will include: an opinion poll on last year's best two stamps, a short history of the society, a "Guess the number of stamps in the jar competition," etc. Our theme for our exhibit this year is "Today's Menu." If you are wondering what this title can mean, well, we'll be very pleased to show you at our stand.

Meetings are held fortnightly, on Saturdays, mostly in members' homes. There is a "social" after alternate meetings. New members are welcome and should contact the Secretary.

Hon. Scretary: Peter Powell, 39 Newlands Road, Tunbridge Wells (Phone 20676).

19) Pictorials For a Brighter Britain Campaign

The Newlands Road Philatelic Society was MOST CERTAINLY one the organisations that helped change the Post Office Stamp Issuing Policy, for in the early 1960s things changed, and we definitely helped that change to happen.

Proof that this is true is in the Post Office's own Website.

But let's start at the beginning. It was seeing this page in Gibbon's Stamp Monthly that inspired us. In

GIBBONS STAMP MONTHLY

EDITED BY C. P. RANG — VOL. XXIX JUNE 1, 1956 No. 10 — PUBLISHED PRICE SIXPENCE NET

G.S.M. EDITOR'S DESIGNS FOR GREAT BRITAIN

See page 127

1959, three years after this article appeared, we decided to try to make it happen. We wrote to Charles P Rang, the Editor of Gibbon's Monthly (he had actually designed one stamp for an African country) asking him about helping his campaign. At this time we had heard nothing more about the campaign. We knew that Viscount Ellibank in the House of Lords was leading the campaign too, and between them they had printed for us 100 copies of these designs on good glossy paper. So in April we had these envelopes printed, and sent a copy of the CP Rang designs to the Postmaster General, the Leaders of each of three parties, and a few others, like Harold Wilson and our own MP, Richard Hornby. These were posted on May 6th

1959. (Anniversary of the 1d Black.)

On the next few pages are scans of the letters we got back from the MPs. Our own MP, Richard Hornby, did write to the Post Office, and sent back the reply he got from them, but made no comments himself. The party leaders all got their secretaries to respond. We

FROM THE
RT. HON. HAROLD WILSON, M.P.

HOUSE OF COMMONS

8th May, 1959.

Dear Mr. Powell,

Thank you for your letter of 6th May, about pictorial stamps for Great Britain.

When I opened the National Stamp Exhibition last year, I made the same plea that your Society is making and my colleague, Mr. Ness Edwards, a former Postmaster General, has pressed the same suggestion from the Opposition Front Bench. I should be very glad to pass your letter on to him, since he is the Labour Party's official spokesman on Post Office affairs.

Yours sincerely,

Harold Wilson.

Mr. Peter Powell,
39, Newlands Road,
Tunbridge Wells,
Kent.

HOUSE OF COMMONS

7th May, 1959.

Dear Mr. Powell,

Mr. Grimond asks me to acknowledge your letter of the 6th May concerning pictorial stamps.

Yours sincerely,

C. Fisher.

Private Secretary

Peter Powell, Esq.,
39, Newlands Road,
Tunbridge Wells,
Kent.

PRIME MINISTER

10 Downing Street
Whitehall

May 11th, 1959

Dear Sir,

I write on behalf of the Prime Minister to thank you for your letter.

Yours truly,

John Wyndham.

The Hon. Secretary,
Newlands Road Philatelic Society.

HOUSE OF COMMONS

PARLIAMENTARY LABOUR PARTY
HOUSE OF COMMONS

HM/CEP 17th July 1959

Dear Mr. Phillips,

Mr. Ness Edwards, M.P., has informed me about your letter of 14th July and you will be glad to know that a question has been addressed to the Postmaster General for answer on Wednesday, 22nd July.

I will write to you again after the matter has been considered in Parliament.

Yours sincerely,

Carol Johnson

Secretary.

C. Phillips, Esq.,
Hon. President,
The Newlands Road Philatelic Society,
15 Newlands Road,
TUNBRIDGE WELLS,
Kent.

also sent a letter to Harold Wilson, later to become Prime Minister; we knew he was in favour as he had officially opened Stampex a few years before, and mentioned pictorials. He wrote back a very nice letter. Several years later in 1967, when he was Prime Minister, he officially opened the new School I was teaching in, Edlington Comprehensive, near Doncaster, and he came to shake hands with all the teaching staff. I asked him if he remembered us writing to him in 1959, and he said he did, and went on to say that the present Postmaster General was making some changes. The other teachers, who had been much longer at the school, were surprised that he talked to ME, a Junior member of the teaching staff……….

The questions asked in Parliament on our behalf by Mr Ness Edwards were reported in Stamp Collecting Weekly and later in the Kent and Sussex Courier. But before that we hit the NATIONAL NEWS-

COLLECTING

July 31st, 1959

EWS EL GE

ASSISTANT P.M.G. AGAIN SAYS "NO" TO PICTORIALS

There were cheers in the House of Commons when Mr. Kenneth Thompson, the Assistant Postmaster-General, urged to " meet the needs of modern society " by issuing pictorial stamps, emphasised that there was no intention of changing the present policy.

Mr. Ness Edwards, a former Postmaster-General, won some vocal support however, when he said that the sample pictorials shown by Viscount Elibank meant that the Post Office's case fell to the ground. He added that the tradition of giving predominance to the sovereign's head had been altered for our high value stamps—so why should it still have to apply to the low values?

Mr. W. R. Williams recalled that Mr. Marples (P.M.G.) had inspected " the excellent and very profitable stamp department in Washington ", and asked why we were trailing behind.

He had the sample pictorial stamps before him, answered Mr. Thompson, but he believed that most people were well satisfied with the present policy. They had given thorough consideration to the whole question—including what was done by other countries—and while there might be some advantages in making a change there were also very real disadvantages.

ELIBANK QUESTION No. 13—AND STILL NO LUCK

Question No. 13 about pictorial stamps for Britain, which he has just asked in the House of Lords, brought Viscount Elibank no more success than any of the previous dozen.

He achieved his " baker's dozen " on the topic which he has made peculiarly his own when he asked if the Postmaster-General had responded to an appeal made earlier this year and prepared designs of small, low value pictorials.

Lord Chesham replied that Mr. Marples had not done so—and added that the Government had no intention of changing the present stamp policy.

House of Commons,
London, S.W.1

28th June 1960.

Dear Mr.Powell,

Thank you for your letter of June 26th. I certainly agree with you that our stamps need to be made more attractive.

I am grateful to you for writing to me, and I will do what I can to help.

Yours sincerely,

Sydney Irving, M.P.

Peter Powell,Esq.,
Secretary,
Newlands Road Philatelic Society,
39, Newlands Road,
Tunbridge Wells,
Kent.

13th May,1959.

Dear Mr. Powell,

I am writing on behalf of Mr. Gaitskell to thank you for your letter of May 6th. He is sorry to hear that you did not get a more satisfactory answer to your petition to the Postmaster General. I know that members of the Parliamentary Labour Party who are specially interested in this subject will shareyour views and Mr. Gaitskell is, therefore, sending your letter to Mr. Ness Edwards, a former Postmaster General, to see whether any action can be taken.

Yours sincerely,

Private Secretary.

Mr. Peter Powell,
39, Newlands Road,
Tunbridge Wells,
Kent.

Our Own M.P.

House of Commons,
London, S.W.1

7th May, 1959

Dear Mr. Powell,

Thank you for your letter about postage stamps. I will try to find out what is the objection of the Post Office. I cannot pretend that this is a subject on which I have any strong feelings.

Yours sincerely,

Richard Hornby

Peter Powell Esq.,
39, Newlands Road,
Tunbridge Wells

House of Commons,
London, S.W.1

2nd June, 1959

Dear Mr. Powell,

I enclose the reply which I have received from the Assistant Postmaster-General, which I think is self-explanatory.

Yours sincerely,

Richard Hornby

Peter Powell Esq.,
39, Newlands Road,
Tunbridge Wells

PAPERS, thanks to the "Observer", Sunday July 19 1959.

As already mentioned in the Chapter on the Hobbies Exhibition, we asked the public to sign a petition,

Kent & Sussex Courier Oct. 2nd 1959

Stamp society gets its reply

The general public are satisfied with the existing postage stamps and there is no demand for a more pictorial design, stated a spokesman for the G.P.O. in a letter to the Newlands Road Philatelic Society. This was read out at its competition meeting at Culverden House on Saturday.

The letter said that since British stamps were first issued in 1840, they have continued to have a high prestige; it was mainly the philatelic societies which asked for pictorial stamps. The economics of printing would not justify the change-over. The G.P.O., however, would be willing to have more pictorial designs on postmarks.

Mr. James Watson, assistant editor of Gibbons's Stamp Monthly, addressed the meeting and presented the prizes to:

Over 13: 1 Christopher Selmes, 2 Patrick Hoyle, 3 Christopher Phillips; under 13: 1 Bronwen Phillips, 2 Patrick Smith, 3 Susan Smith; thematic prize: Simon Levett; best new member: John Seymen.

THE OBSERVER, SUNDAY, JULY 19, 1959

TABLE TALK

Election Issue

THE Government is under fire from an unusual quarter. The perennial campaign for pictorial postage stamps has now been taken up by the Newlands Road Philatelic Society, in the Tory heart of Tunbridge Wells. The president of the society, nineteen-year-old CHRISTOPHER PHILLIPS, has been vigorously attacking the Postmaster-General, MR. MARPLES, in the *Newlands Post*, "printed on the Skinner's School duplicator, kindly lent by the headmaster, MR. C. H. BEEBY, M.A."

Mr. Phillips has been sending to the P.M.G. samples of pictorial stamps—advocated by Viscount

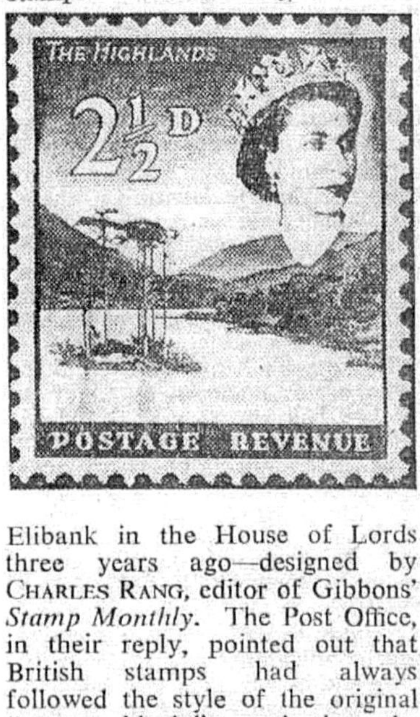

Elibank in the House of Lords three years ago—designed by CHARLES RANG, editor of Gibbons' *Stamp Monthly*. The Post Office, in their reply, pointed out that British stamps had always followed the style of the original "penny black": and that the presence of the Monarch's portrait gave Britain the "unique privilege," allowed by the Universal Postal Convention, of not having to include the name of the country.

As the average age of the Newlands Road Philatelic Society is about thirteen, Mr. Marples may well have a long war on his hands.

G.P.O. HEADQUARTERS,
ST. MARTIN'S LE GRAND,
LONDON, E.C.1.

TELEPHONE: HEADQUARTERS 4020

From the Assistant Postmaster General

1st June ~~May~~, 1959.

My dear Hornby,

You wrote to me on the 7th May forwarding the enclosed letter you had received from Mr. Peter Powell, the Secretary of the Newlands Road Philatelic Society, about pictorial postage stamps.

As we have explained in separate correspondence with Mr. Powell, it is our policy to have a basic series of stamps for each reign, commonly remaining unchanged throughout the reign, supplemented from time to time by special stamps to mark outstanding current events or postal or royal anniversaries. The style and general appearance of the basic issue was set by the original British postage stamp - the Penny Black - and we still keep to its simple dignity, with the Monarch's head as the dominent feature, for all our low value stamps (up to 1/6d.). The present high value stamps (2/6d. to £1) are, however, larger and include in their design pictures of four famous castles (Carrickfergus, Caernarvon, Edinburgh and Windsor) in addition to the portrait of the Queen.

To go further than this and include pictorial themes in our low value stamps is, I think, impracticable in such small sized stamps if we are to include the Queen's portrait in such a way that it is the dominent feature of the design. The Queen's portrait is the indication of origin of our stamps and we alone of all postal administrations have not been called on to include the name of the country in them as the Universal Postal Convention requires all countries to do. As you can well appreciate we value this privilege very highly and would not willingly abandon it. We could not consider the alternative of making the stamps bigger as we know that business firms like our small-sized stamps, and all our 18,000 or so stamp selling machines are designed to take this particular size.

We have given careful consideration to the desirability of altering this many times but have come to the conclusion that it would be wrong that in stamps for everyday use we should depart from the honoured and accepted tradition that the Queen's head should be the dominent theme.

The Newlands Road Philatelic Society are not original in seeking to raise the question of pictorials in the House. It has been discussed both in the Commons and, in response to questions from Viscount Elibank, in the Lords.

Will you please ask Mr. Powell to accept this letter as a reply to his other letters sent direct to the Prime Minister, the Postmaster General, and myself.

Yours ever,

Lord Mancroft

asking for small pictorial postage stamps. We had over 100 willing people to sign. This is a scan of a copy of the PO reply that was in The Newlands Post of July 1959.

The number of times F J Langfield had to write

General Post Office,
Postal Services Department,
St. Martin's-le-Grand,
LODON, E.C.1.

Dear Sir, 20th April 1959.

The Postmaster General has asked me to thank you for your letter and petition of the 11th April.

I should perhaps explain a little of the background to our stamp policy. We have a basic issue of stamps for each reign, commonly remaining unchanged throughout the reign, supplemented from time to time by special stamps to mark outstanding current events or postal or royal anniversaries. The style and general appearance of the basic issue was set by the original British postage stamp - The Penny Black - and with pride we still keep to its simple dignity, with the Monarch's head as the dominant feature, for all our low value stamps (up to 1/6). The present high value stamps (2/6 - £1) are, as you know, larger and include in their design pictures of four castles in addition to the portrait of the Queen. The special issues are usually twice the size of the basic issues; they also always include the portrait of the Monarch together with some theme associated with the event being marked.

You would like us to change the design of our basic low value stamps and include illustrations of Britains beauty spots in them instead. We do not think it practicable to do this in such small sized stamps and also to include the Monarch's head in such a way that it is the dominant feature of the design. I think you will agree that even in Mr. C.P. Rang's designs this is still the case. The Monarch's portrait is the indication that our stamps are British and we alone of all postal administrations have not been called on to include the name of the country in our stamps as the Universal Postal Convention requires all countries to do. We value this privilege very highly and I am sure you would not wish to suggest that we should omit such a delightful method of demonstrating the country of origin of our stamp. We could not consider the alternative of making the stamps bigger as we know that business firms like our small sized stamps, and all our 18000 or so stamp selling machines are designed to take this particular size.

I hope this explains the position to you. Although therefore we cannot adopt the suggestion we nevertheless appreciate your Society's interest in writing to us.

Yours faithfully,
F.J. Langfield. (signed).

that letter to us, in slightly different words must have been rather frustrating for him!

The following year we went at them even harder; we had another petition, and this time 335 people signed. An opinion poll showed 93% in favour of small pictorial stamps out of 359 voters, and this time we wrote to all the Kent MPs with a copy of C P Rang's designs. Sydney Irving (one of the Kent MPs) did write

From Viscount Elibank, CMG. DSO.

602 Carrington House

Hertford Street, W. 1

May 12, 1959

Mr Peter Powell
Hon. Secretary
Newlands Road Philatelic Society
39 Newlands Road,
Tunbridge Wells, Kent.

Dear Mr Powell,

SMALL, LOW VALUES, PICTORIAL STAMPS.

I was very glad to receive your letter of May 6th, signed also by Messrs Phillips and Hoyte. The attitude of three Post Masters General towards my long campaign for Small Pictorials, namely, Earl De Le Warr, Dr. Charles Hill, M.P. (the erstwhile Radio Docter), and Mr Ernest Marples, M.P., is scandalous and does them the greatest discredit. The envelope which you sent me is excellent, and I am very glad to know that you are continuing to send copies to the P.M.G., though whether the bureaucrats at the Post Office ever allow them to reach him personally is another matter, and is open to doubt. I wish you and your Society the greatest success in your National Campaign for Pictorials for a Brighter Britain. It occurs to me that I might be able to help you in this by asking Mr C.P. Rang - of Messrs Stanley, Gibbons & Co. who designed the small pictorials* which I exhibited in the House of Lords when advocating these stamps in a speech on May 16, 1956 - whether he would kindly lend you the block from which the designs were made. You and your colleagues can think this over, and communicate with me at your leisure.

Yours sincerely

Elibank

May 13 Since writing above, I have had a phone talk with Mr Rang, the outcome of which is as follows, He will kindly have a block made of the above * small pictorials and have a few hundred reproductions made from the block which I will purchase from him and present to [illegible] in your campaign in whatever way you wish.

back a nice positive reply. Only 8 of the 18 Kent MPs bothered to reply; whilst 4 at least passed on the letters to Mr Hornby, the rest ignored them. One other reasonable reply came from Julian Critchley (Rochester & Chatham), who only PARTLY agreed with us, and Mr John Wells, MP for Maidstone, took up the question with the PMG, and got a reply similar to the one we did. Mr Bill Deedes, MP for Ashford, said the

HOUSE OF COMMONS

PARLIAMENTARY LABOUR PARTY

HOUSE OF COMMONS

HM/CEP

23rd July 1959

Dear Mr. Phillips,

The proposal regarding pictorial stamps was raised in the House of Commons yesterday as a result of Questions put down by Labour Members.

I am enclosing extracts from Hansard, from which you will observe that the Government are not prepared to make any change. I am very sorry, but it seems there is really nothing further we can do at the present time.

Yours sincerely,

Carol Johnson

Secretary.

C. Phillips, Esq.,
Hon. President,
The Newlands Road Philatelic Society,
15 Newlands Road,
TUNBRIDGE WELLS,
Kent.

See next Page for the Hansard page.,

POST OFFICE

Low-Value Stamps (Design)

4. **Mr. Ness Edwards** asked the Postmaster-General if he will now consider the issue of low-value pictorial stamps.

7. **Mr. W. R. Williams** asked the Postmaster-General whether he will consider breaking away from the traditional form of low-value postage stamps and issue them with pictorial designs.

Mr. K. Thompson: I have gone into this matter very thoroughly. I believe most people are well satisfied with our policy of maintaining the present size of our low-value stamps and giving predominance on them to the portrait of the Queen. I do not propose to change it.

Mr. Edwards: As the old practice has been breached in the case of the high-value stamps, surely there is a case for meeting the general interest which is shown by the young people of this country by giving an opportunity to buy low-value stamps which carry pictorial descriptions? Is the hon. Member aware that in another place examples of stamps were submitted which did not interfere with the tradition of having the Queen's head on the stamp and did not increase the size of the stamp? In view of that fact, does it not appear that his case falls to the ground?

Mr. Thompson: I have before me examples of the stamps to which the right hon. Gentleman refers. The main considerations which we have to take into account are, first, that it would be highly inconvenient to both business users and the Post Office to alter the size of the stamps; and, secondly, that having decided to maintain the present size of the low-value stamps, it does not seem to us to be possible to have a pictorial design together with a proper representation of the portrait of the Qu[illegible].

Copy of the relevant Hansard pages asked on our behalf.

Mr. W. R. Williams: Is the Minister aware that I do not think that there is anything at all in the last arg[illegible]nt? Is it not quite practicable to do anything we like with stamps provided that we have the right ideas about them? Is it not correct that the Postmaster-General, like myself, had the opportunity to see that excellent and indeed very profitable stamp department in Washington? Why are we trailing behind other countries in our stamp issue? Will the Minister ask his right hon. Friend to ask the advisory committee to look at some of these examples to see whether they cannot be less conservative than some hon. Members who have been hailing the Minister this afternoon?

Mr. Thompson: We have considered these various matters, including the experience of other authorities. While there may be some advantages in making changes, there are real disadvantages, and we do not want to take those over from the American or other authorities.

Dame Florence Horsbrugh: Does my right hon. Friend realise that many people do not want these changes, nor do they want the tradition broken? Am I right in saying that we are the only country in the world which has the Sovereign's head so clearly portrayed that it does not include the name of the country on the stamp?

Mr. Thompson: My right hon. Friend is perfectly correct. Our position in that respect arises from the fact that we were the first people to use stamps and that we are not required to put on the stamp the name of the country. We do not want to lose that position.

Mr. Edwards: Is not the Minister aware that the specimen stamps exhibited in the other place interfered neither with the size of the stamp nor with the position, nor did they leave the Queen's head off the stamps? Is he aware that in that way tradition is preserved and we meet the needs of modern society?

Mr. Thompson: That is one opinion with which I cannot agree.

"THE PICTORIAL STAMPS BRITAIN OUGHT TO HAVE" (by Susan Smith)

(NOTE. This essay was writen for the Haworth Memorial Competition in Febuary and was given 75% - but did not win a prize. Only two entries were sent up for this competition, the other entry being by Christopher Phillips, from the N.R.P.S. More entries are expected this year - the subject has still to be announced.) (Unfortuneatly the illustrative stamps cannot be shewn).

Why shouldn't Britain have pictorial stamps??

How much more interesting other countries' envelopes are, owing to the fact that they issue pictorials, in a variety of colours in a style similar to Ruanda - Urundi. Another reason that makes pictorials so neccessary for Britain is that we were the first country to issue stamps, therefore we should be ahead and influencing the rest of the world, not just sitting back and waiting for them to influence us in stamp designs.

I am also convinced that when Sir Rowland Hill annunciated the first postage stamp he did not expect the same principle to be in use 122 years later, though he would probably be flattered, but times have changed in all subjects, but not so in the stamps of Great Britain.

The Queen's head on stamps is very pleasing and traditional, but very unimaginative. The Monarch's head should however not be abolished completely. St. Helena, for one country, has overcome this problem admirably, (The design shewn is one of Mr. C.P. Rang's ... Ed.) The fish depicted on this issue are found on the coast of St. Helena, and the Queen's head is depicted in the corner, adding an unique touch to the stamps that only countries in the British Commonwealth are priviledged to use.

If it is argued that machinery has to be adjusted at a large cost, I cannot see that there is any more difficulty than on the rare occaisons that pictorial commemorative stamps have been issued, in similar fashion to that of St. Helena.

In Britain there is a wide variety of subjects that could be used to make some interesting sets. British nature would make a very good basis as there is a wide selection of typically English birds, flowers, trees, and animals.

A set with robin, wren, thrush, finches, blackbird and etc. would be an attractive and appropiate. For flowers, in addition to wild flowers, a wonderful set could be made of the English rose, with its wide varieties and colours. There are a number of wild animals such as the fox, deer, squirrel and badger. There is also a large number of fine trees that are typically English. Both of these would make delightful sets.

(Susan then showed three stamps of other countries, and compared it with 'our feeble effort')

Britain's industry could be the theme for other sets, as also could farming. Britain has had many disinguished people of the arts. Not only painters, but writers, poets, composers, dancers and actors. These could all be split into categories and featured under different headings.

Around England there are many famous landmarks and buildings that would illustrate Britain's beauty. Stonehenge and the Houses of Parliament are two examples.

Yes Britain must definitely have pictorial stamps in the very near future. Not just on high value parcel-post stamps, in one dull colour, but in a wide variety of stamps in a wide range of colours.

Susan Smith wrote this for the Haworth Memorial Competition run by the World Association Of Young stamp Collectors. She did not win, but it was published in the Newlands Post. July 1962.

present design was not very good, but better than the £1 note!

By 1962/3, the post office was issuing more commemorative stamps, and ones in multicolour, and with pictorial designs. So when we had our 10th anniversary public exhibition in the art club rooms, on the Pantiles, in July 1963, we had a larger than usual Newlands Post, and it included a page praising the Post Office for their more relaxed policies. The only thing remaining was having small, low value definitives, which they have stubbornly refused to do, except for a few Christmas stamps in recent years.

Kenneth Chapman even wrote us a letter confirming that he thought that **our** efforts had had a decisive

Stamp Collecting LIMITED

PHILATELIC PUBLISHERS

DIRECTORS:
T. W. HODGSON (GOVERNING)
D. B. ARMSTRONG
C. F. HODGSON
H. PARSONS
K. F. CHAPMAN (EDITORIAL)

PUBLICATION: "STAMP COLLECTING" WEEKLY
INCORPORATING "STAMP REVIEW"
Founded 1913
Tel.: TEMple Bar 2684 & 7814

KFC/EIW.

42 MAIDEN LANE
LONDON, W.C.2

5th December, 1963.

Christopher Phillips, Esq.,
5 Tavistock Road,
Sketty,
Swansaea,
Glamorgan.

Dear Christopher Phillips,

We quite agree with the sentiments expressed in your letter of December 2nd. The British Post Office has done quite a lot to aid philatelists and it may well be that before many years have passed we shall find ourselves with British pictorial stamps. If we do, you and your friends of the Newlands Road Philatelic Society will have played no small part in ensuring their issue.

Yours sincerely,

Kenneth F Chapman

EDITOR.

-15-

G.P.O. GIVES WAY TO 8/9ths OF OUR DEMANDS

PHILATELIC HISTORY has been made by the British Post Office this year; this we know, is partly due to our Society's own efforts, in fact a hard fought three year campaign. During these three years the N.R.P.S. did the following:-

Sent up two petitions to Parliament.

Wrote to leading Parliamentarians (Two P.M.G.'s, Harold MacMillan Prime Minister; Jo Grimond, leader of Liberal Party; Mr. Gaitskell, then leader of Labour Party; Harold Wilson - who sent personal replie and Viscount Ellibank.)

WHY NOT?

Wrote to all the Kent M.P.'s.

And Conducted an Opinion Poll - result : 90% in favour of pictorials

All these letters urged the G.P.O. to issue small low value pictorials, of the type illustrated here (design by Charles Rang, Editor G.S.M.)

In addition Christopher Phillips wrote many letters to the P.M.G.s, Mr. Hornby M.P., and Mr. Langfield (Postal Services Dept.). These letters again stood up for the 'Pictorials for brighter Britain Campaign', and in addition he tried to persuade the G.P.O. to issue better designed commemorative stamps with more imagination; to publicise new issues of stamps well in advance, to set up a Philatelic Bureau, and to reverse the date and slogan positioning of machine cancellations. Christopher also suggested that many National events were being missed, and also that more use should be made of pictorial slogan cancellations.

Replies from the G.P.O. were always the same, 'We have considered it, but have decided against any change'. Apparently our suggestions and demands were falling upon deaf ears. We gave it a rest for two years. Then soon after a new assistant P.M.G. had been appointed, a complete change occured! Coincidence? This year has seen the issue of more commemorative stamps than ever before, they were given wide publicity, they are in attractive modern designs, and are pictorial in some cases (some in FIVE COLOURS!). That is not all, for a G.P.O. Philatelic Bureau has been set up (and this includes a First Day Cover service - rather expensive!), and now several holiday towns are being able to use special pictorial postmarks (Including Tunbridge Wells), and in Bath the positioning of the slogan and date have been reversed!

Almost a small pictorial!

Neo-pictorial

This and the next page is a scan of the article that appeared in the 10th anniversary Newlands Post, re our successes.

influence on the Post Office's change of direction.

That does not mean we now agree with the present 1990s onwards massive increase in new Special stamps. From the beginning of the millennium, the quantity and cost of new issues has spiralled out of all

CONGRATULATIONS TO THE G.P.O.

This means that eight out of nine things we asked for have been granted. The ninth, the one we consider the most imprtnt, still needs to be fought for; that is SMALL DEFINITIVE PICTORIALS

This is a great victory for the N.R.P.S. although, of course the N.R.P.S. cannot take even the majority of the credit, for this campaign was begun years ago by people like Viscount Ellinbank, nevertheless the N.R.P.S. must have helped this wonderful change by the G.P.O.

This new break-away has now given rise to a commemorative set of stamps for Shakespeare. The announcement of how the G.P.O. were able to do this without breaking their traditions, which **gave rise to a classic historical statement:-**

- "The Post Office said that their special issue of stamps on April 23rd 1964 - 400th **Anniversary** of the birth of William Shakespeare - will not be commemorating either Shakespeare or his anniversary, the reason for their issue is TO MARK THE COMMEMORATION CELEBRATIONS." -

This statement is surely a remarkable way of issuing a set of stamps for an event without really doing it!.

Our campaign for low value pictorials will continue; for having got this far, it would be stupid to give up for our last demand. EVERYONE can help by writing to the G.P.O.

TRUE PICTORIALS

A STUDENT OPINION POLL conducted at the Medway College of Technology last September, and published in their Students' Union Newspaper MeOFT showed 77% of the students in favour of small low value pictorial postage stamps, 20% were against, and only 3% didn't know.

control, and has taken away the fun of collecting British stamps.

Now coming to modern times, I was pleasantly surprised to see that our campaign is now recognised by the Post Office itself, because I found in the Postal Museum copies of our letters to the Post Office. Here is a picture of the web page.

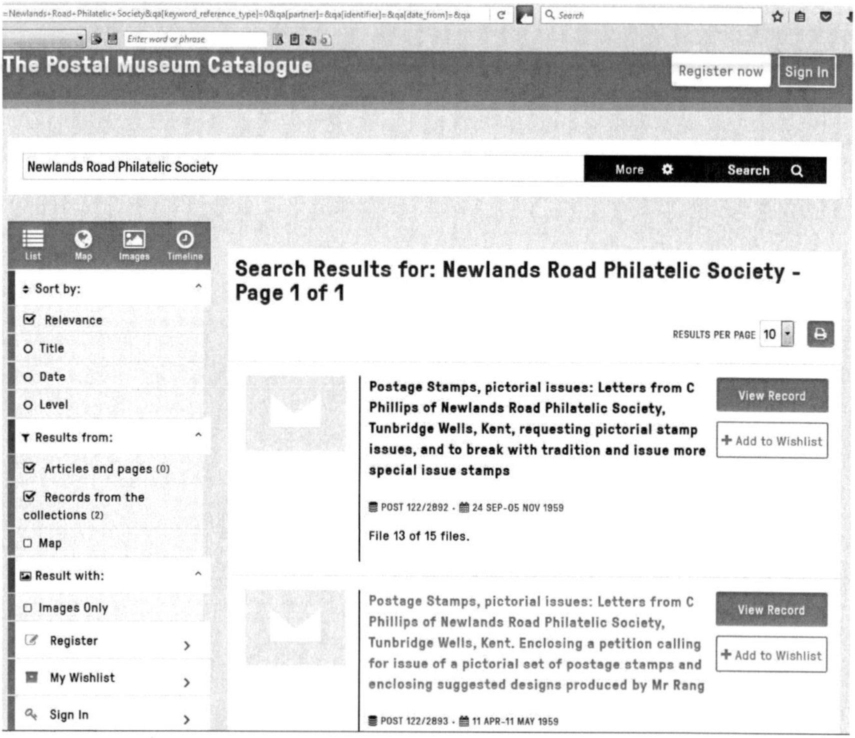

One further matter I must mention is the extensive correspondence that took place in the Letters pages of “Stamp Collecting Weekly”. It started off with this letter from July 31st 1959, and there were still letters as a result up until the end of the year. I will post a few of them here. One of the most important ones came from Charles P Rang, the designer of the samples, and Editor of Gibbons’ Stamp Monthly. One of the most against the idea was Ian T Hamilton. That prompted a great reply from one of our own members, Christopher Selmes (see next page), and a few other heated responses, including one from Ian T Hamilton himself. Later, the magazine published an article about French Stamps, by Ian T Hamilton, which prompted me to write what was a final posting on the subject. As a result he was invited to give a display at our society, which he accepted Feb 18th 1961.

I have posted the full minutes of that meeting.

July 31st, 1959 *STAMP COL*

"Quoting You"

Opinions expressed are not necessarily endorsed by the Editor

PICTORIALS FOR BRITAIN

SIR,—This society is proposing to start a national campaign for small low-value pictorial stamps for Great Britain. It will, of course, need the support of a large number of people. We would be prepared to have printed special covers, say for the 120th anniversary of the Penny Black, which supporters could send to their M.P.s, the P.M.G. and also use as ordinary envelopes. Stamp dealers, if interested, could use them for their business transactions. We believe that if enough people wrote to their M.P.s and the G.P.O. then the P.M.G. would have to take some notice.

Our arguments are based on those of Lord Elibank. The Post Office claim that ever since they issued the world's first stamp they have kept to the same style and general appearance, but we are sure that most stamp collectors will agree with us when we say that *no* British stamp of the same size as the Penny Black has come up to its standard. The type of designs we have in mind are those produced by Mr. C. P. Rang for Lord Elibank's campaign in the House of Lords. (*Illustrated above*)

Anyone willing to support us by buying any special covers which we might produce is invited to write to the undersigned. Letters requiring a reply should be accompanied by a stamped addressed envelope.

CHRISTOPHER PHILLIPS,
Newlands Road P.S.

15 Newlands Road,
Tunbridge Wells, Kent.

SIR,—Why is it that whenever I am abroad someone takes advantage of the situation and writes to the Press demanding the introduction of pictorial stamps? I returned home a few days ago to find (STAMP COLLECTING, July 31st) some lunatic society decrying the present-day portrait of the reigning monarch, and in the same breath proposing a campaign for *pictorial* stamps supported by a " printed special cover, say for the 120th anniversary of the Penny Black ", i.e. a cover celebrating *a non-pictorial issue*! This is surely an admission that the Newlands Road P.S. has no faith in its own war cry!

It does not seem to be realised that photogravure is a cheap process, and its products are equally cheap in appearance unless possibly handled by a Courvoisier. A photograph lacks the inspiration of the artist. Furthermore, there are no good designers in this country—our best are mediocre compared with, say, those that France possesses. All that the " Rang Essays " do is to symbolise a decapitated monarchy (the Teddy Boy Republic) and point out the difficulties of designing a pictorial stamp. The Queen's head springing out of the hillside in the 2½d. value illustrates particularly well the problem, without solving it.

If your correspondent would devote his attention to the stamps of modern France and study them for a change, he would realise that the more expensive process of (line) engraving and a different-sized format is necessary for successful results. He might also ask himself whether Republican France would be able to be so successful if it had to suffer the inclusion of a monarch's likeness. Likewise, Courvoisier's best efforts are republican in nature.

Finally, with all respect to Mr. Rang, is it not dangerous to " plug " a set of stamps designed by someone connected with the trade? Might it not lead to another Marconi scandal? In his own interests, Mr. Rang should dissociate himself from these designs.

Ewell, Surrey. IAN T. HAMILTON.

"PICTORIALS FOR BRITAIN"

The argument centred around the desirability, or otherwise, of pictorial stamps for Great Britain received a shot in the arm with the publication, on July 31st, of a letter from Christopher Phillips, of Tunbridge Wells, inviting support for a campaign favouring the issue of pictorials.

Ian T. Hamilton expressed contrary views in " Quoting You " on September 18th. Here is Christopher Phillips's reply to Mr. Hamilton, some observations from Charles P. Rang, sponsor in the philatelic press of the " Elibank Essays ", and certain other forthright letters on this topic.

* * * *

SIR,—I must apologise for writing whilst Mr. Hamilton was enjoying his holiday in that "decapitated monarchy" France, and if Mr. Hamilton would be so good as to let us know when he is at home I will endeavour to write in future at a more convenient time. Could we also leave the mud-slinging to politicians?

Although we are going hammer-and-tongs against the P.M.G. on the question of pictorials, we believe that we have the best, most efficient and cheapest Post Office in the world, and that it could do even better if it bowed to public opinion.

In 1840 Britain led the world in postage stamps, and the idea for special covers for the 120th anniversary does not show that we have no faith in our campaign but how we in Britain lag behind.

Our present stamps may well give the impression that Britain hasn't any good designers, but what chance have we if there is no competition? A few people are chosen, told what to put on the stamp and the best (if we can call it the best) design is used.

Even people who do not want pictorials (including Government officials in the Lords) agree that Mr. Rang's designs are quite nice, and with a few alterations they would make a very pleasant change from the squiggles we have to put up with at present.

Although we agree with the letter from Mr. Davis on some points, we think that it would be impossible to do as he suggests, as the big business firms would, according to the Post Office, object to larger stamps, and that there might be a public outcry if the Queen's portrait were removed.

Readers can support the campaign by writing to the papers, the P.M.G., their M.P. and, if possible, organise a petition in their local philatelic society. We want British stamps, not French.

Tunbridge Wells, Kent. CHRISTOPHER PHILLIPS.

SIR,—I do sympathise with Mr. Ian T. Hamilton's finding that the " Pictorial " enthusiasts have been at it again while he was gallivanting on the Continent. But I hope that he will commiserate with me in having to rise from my sick-bed and tap out with one finger—of the left hand at that—these few comments on his effusion which you published in STAMP COLLECTING of September 18th.

Fancy saying that there are no good stamp designers in this country! I hope that the members of our stamp-printing firms will surmount their usual modesty and point out to Mr. Hamilton what they (and their predecessors) have been doing in the last 100 years. There are also many other artists in the commercial world who could show him a thing or two if only they received more encouragement from the Post Office.

And that other letter of Mr. Reginald W. Davis, in the same number of STAMP COLLECTING, which calmly suggests that we should dispense with the portrait of the Queen, just in order to have an entirely pictorial stamp! There seems to be some topsy-turvy thinking here. The whole intention of pictorial stamps is that they should add to the prestige of this country. The possession of a monarch is still, in the opinion of most people, our No. 1 asset. Our national monuments, historic scenes and beauty spots fall in various positions down the list of assets. Therefore, the Queen's portrait comes first and must remain an indispensable feature of our postage stamps. It's the squiggles and needless decoration which are no asset at all that we ask should be thrown out to give room for suitable pictorial subjects.

It is not necessary that the Queen's portrait should be reduced to negligible proportions. The " Elibank-Rang " designs in which *none of the heads were smaller than in the current low values* proved this. Another purpose of those designs was to show that a combination of portrait and picture could be more attractive than a combination of portrait and squiggles. Many people thought that they proved the point. If a mere editor could do that much, then proper designers should be able to do even better.

In one respect Mr. Hamilton and I agree, that is on the poor quality of our photogravure. But this is no fault of our printers, but merely due to the parsimonious attitude of the Post Office. You don't find our national advertisers cutting down on printing and paper.

Finally, what kind of scandal does Mr. Hamilton think I am likely to run into? I have merely sided with one of our livelier peers in asking for better stamps for this country, and as a philatelic editor I feel as qualified as anybody to air such views. Anyone would think I had been peddling opium to children!

CHARLES P. RANG

(Editor, Gibbons' Stamp Monthly).

SIR,—I have read with utter dismay and amazement the letter from Mr. Ian T. Hamilton. I am very surprised that such remarks should come from a man of Mr. Hamilton's standing. He asks why, in his absence, someone writes to the press demanding pictorial stamps for Britain. Well, Mr. Hamilton, the answer is perfectly clear and always will be. It is because pictorial stamps *are* required in this country and until we get these decently designed, and printed in at least two colours, a vigorous campaign for such must, and will be, constantly waged, until our stubborn and Victorian-minded Post Office and Government realise that postage stamps are not just little bits of paper to be stuck on envelopes to pay for postal services and then be horribly cancelled with unnecessary and large wavy lines which form part of the modern postmark.

No society or individual is lunatic-minded who decries our present ugly and uninspiring one-colour photogravure atrocities known as postage stamps, and it is up to *every* individual, whether he is a stamp collector or not, to support Lord Elibank's campaign for pictorial stamps.

Mr. Hamilton states : " . . . photogravure is a cheap process, and its products are equally cheap." Well, Mr. Hamilton, you should know that cheapness never pays, and anyway, why should cheapness enter into the question at all? What we want are good pictorial stamps, finely engraved and printed and, as you refer to modern French as an example, what could be better? If, as you say, we haven't any good designers in this country then we must go to France for them ; as for format, well change it, and make all our stamps the same size as the current high values, and then we can have our Queen's portrait in as well, and if the powers that be make the excuse that they haven't enough money to justify decently-designed and printed stamps, then the money should be taken from one of the several projects where it is already being wasted on unnecessary and unwanted schemes.

Finally, Mr. Hamilton, if I remember rightly, in reports in STAMP COLLECTING (" Society Nights ") I read of " Tripe from the Dustbin " by Ian Hamilton. This time it appears to be " Tripe from Hamilton "—and utter tripe at that!

Hitchin, Herts. R. J. CANNON.

Oct 9th 1959 Stamp Collecting Weekly page 143

SIR,—I cannot see the reason for the outburst of calumny by Mr. Ian T. Hamilton. He appears to have overlooked the fact that we do not decry the present-day portrait of the monarch, but seek to abolish the deplorable emblems that have plagued our stamps for over 70 years. His remark that Mr. Rang's stamps " symbolise a decapitated monarchy " goes well with his love of French stamps, with their unending chateaux which also symbolise a decapitated monarchy.

Finally, I would like to know what he means by the " Teddy Boy Republic ", and would like to point out that prior to publication of his letter my society (*Newlands Road P.S.*) knew nothing either of Mr. Hamilton or of his peregrinations about Europe.

Tunbridge Wells, Kent. CHRISTOPHER SELMES.

Nov 6th 1959

"PICTORIALS FOR BRITAIN"

SIR,—Just because I go abroad for a short while, I find myself the victim of nearly three columns of vituperation from your readers. I fail to understand why!

Mr. Cannon levels his guns at me and suggests that stamps are "not just little bits of paper to pay for postal services and then be horribly cancelled . . .". Then in heaven's name, *what did Rowland Hill want*? Or does he mean that a pictorial stamp will provide a better postal service than a non-pictorial?

Mr. Phillips wants British stamps, *not French*. How then would he propose to prepay postage if he was domiciled in France? Surely the present arrangement of British *and* French stamps is quite satisfactory?

Mr. Noble seems to have an understanding of the purpose of postage stamps. Unlike Mr. Selmes, he wants his letters delivered the next day, and not delayed because of philatelic enthusiasts sending over-stamped, but first day, covers to themselves, thus delaying postal traffic.

To Mr. Rang I offer my apologies for getting him out of bed (Why is it that all Editors go to bed?). My congratulations to him on his fair-mindedness in presenting both sides of the question. He has, however, overlooked the possibility of pictorial opium pills: the children would love them.

I must confess that Mr. Selmes has every reason never to have heard of me and my peregrinations. Obviously he never reads his STAMP COLLECTING thoroughly, and I have not yet appeared on television. Equally "prior to publication of his letter" I had never heard of Mr. Selmes or his Francophobe Filatelic Society in Tunbridge Wells. Perhaps he would tell us more about it?

Tripe House, Epsom. IAN T. HAMILTON.

Dec 25th 1959

PICTORIALS FOR BRITAIN

SIR,—For the past six or seven years my Association has been pressing for the introduction of "Pictorials for Britain". A survey of the letters received from members indicates that only one anti-pictorialist has come forward.

Why is this? Surely, because pictorials are wanted by the majority of collectors, not only in our own country but in the Dominions, Colonies, Protectorates and other parts of our Commonwealth. Even from behind the "Iron Curtain" come letters expressing surprise that the suggested pictorials have not yet become fact.

Much as I and my fellow-members feel in regard to the desirability for pictorials, I also feel that it is only right that the question should be argued fully.

I am afraid, however, that I must come out on the side of Mr. Ian T. Hamilton as he, being a free British subject, has the right to express his opinions freely (libel and slander excepted) even though his ideas may be antagonistic to those held by the majority of his fellow-countrymen (and women).

Further, Mr. Hamilton is too well-known in the world of philately to have his opinion ignored and I, for one, find no hint of an "outburst of calumny" which apparently upset Mr. Selmes. It seems a pity that Mr. Selmes did not make enquiries as to the standing of Mr. Hamilton before committing his society and himself.

So let us now settle down peacefully to the real job of getting "Pictorials for Britain" and let everyone have his say.

Twickenham, Middx. H. E. PEARSE
(Hon. Secretary, The World Association of Young Stamp Collectors).

NO PICTORIALS, PLEASE!

SIR,—I have read the recent correspondence on the subject of commemorative and pictorial stamps for Great Britain, and I must say I am very pleased the G.P.O. has no intention of changing its policy.

Our present stamps show dignity and style pleasing to look at—and make all other foreign ornamental labels look cheap. I think it would be a great pity to depart from our tradition and descend to the level of such stamp-producing countries as the U.S.A. and France who issue so many pictorial labels in the course of a year.

Surely the chief reason why some stamp collectors would like this to come about is because they would more easily be able to fill up their stamp albums!

Bridport, Dorset. FRANK STAFF.

SIR,—Congratulations to Mr. Ian T. Hamilton on his excellent article on French stamps and his travels in France (STAMP COLLECTING, December 4th). It is articles such as his that keep stamp collecting alive; there is more to stamps than just sticking them in albums and looking for flaws.

Congratulations, also, for helping to prove why Britain should have pictorials. Mr. Hamilton's article is an excellent example of how stamps can, and do, advertise another country. If the French travel agency did not pay him for the article, then they ought to have done so. When will the British Post Office realise what a vast free advertising medium they are missing by their stupid traditionalism. Not only would millions of pictures of historical Britain be sent to every part of the world, but also people would write "three-page articles" on recent visits illustrated by stamps and postmarks, not only in the British stamp magazines but also in the numerous Commonwealth and foreign magazines.

Tunbridge Wells. CHRISTOPHER PHILLIPS
President, Newlands Road P.S.

(P.S.—We are asking Mr. Hamilton to give our society a display in the near future.)

The Minutes of the 210th Meeting of the Newlands Road Philatelic Society.

The meeting was held at Culverden House on February 18th at 3.0.p.m.

The minutes of the last meeting were read, and confirmed by the Acting Chairman Pete Veness. The secretary read a letter from Mr. L. Ash who had given 14/- to the society's funds. It was announced that Patrick Hoyles entry in the ~~Atelville~~ Wilfrid Haworth Memorial Competition was highly commended.

Pete Veness then introduced Mr. Ian T. Hamilton who then gave a most interesting talk on Stamp printing. He talked about the four methods of printing and illustrated his talk with models, diagrams and several forms of printing plates.

Mr Hamilton was thanked by Christopher Phillips.

The meeting closed at 4.15. pm. with 12, members and 2 visitors present.

Signed.
Pete Powell
(Hon Secretary)

R. Lehmus
vice-president.

20) Press Coverage.

We were very proud of our press coverage, and we realised how helpful it was in our success.

Apart from the four stamp magazines: Stamp Collectors Fortnightly, Stamp Collecting Weekly, Philatelic Magazine (Fortnightly) and Gibbons Stamp Monthly, our other regular appearance was in the local weekly newspaper, the Kent & Sussex Courier. We also appeared in the Tunbridge Wells Advertiser (Weekly) and had odd mentions in the national "Children's Newspaper", "Boys' Own" and an Italian Philatelic Magazine, and also one appearance in the Sunday Observer. We also had one mention on BBC local Radio.

The very first of our press coverage:

Order, Gentlemen. We had just been reading *The Newlands Post,* the annual "Newsletter" of the Newlands Road Philatelic Society. This is a Junior Club, entirely run by juniors, and a very lively affair it is, judging from the magazine. Here is a bit of advice from the President, which, if what we are told is correct, might be taken to heart by certain members of adult Societies. President Colin Fowle writes "Many of you play about, others don't . . . so those who play about, even if they have paid their sub., will be thrown out of the meeting until they can act their age".

Stamp Collectors Fortnightly, 26 May 1956

Stamp Collecting Weekly Jul 6th '56

The **Newlands Road P.S.** is a newer organisation formed in April 1953. Once again the Tunbridge Wells Philatelic Society lend a hand, but the programmes of meetings is largely run by the members themselves under the direction of Christopher Phillips, the Honorary Secretary. Competitions, quizzes, treasure hunts and the like provide variety in the programme and keep the society active. On the occasion of the 50th meeting the Mayoress of Royal Tunbridge Wells presented the prizes won in the fifth competition held during the season just closed. The winners were:— 1st, Virginia Timmis; 2nd, Peter Powell; 3rd, Simon Timmis. In the 1956 Melville competition Peter Powell, Susan Smith, Patrick Hoyte and Christopher Phillips won prizes in the local eliminating competition. Membership is open to boys from the age of nine and girls from the age of ten.

Our 1st report in Gibbons Stamp Monthly, July 1957

YOUNG JOURNALISTS

OFTEN in these notes I give news of enterprising juniors who belong to stamp clubs (or "philatelic societies" if you want to be grown up!) supervised by kind-hearted adults but rarely do I hear of clubs run entirely by youngsters themselves with their own president and officers, and their very own (annual) magazine with its appointed editor and sub-editor. Such is the Newlands Road Philatelic Society of Tunbridge Wells, whose hon. secretary and treasurer, Christopher Phillips, has kindly sent me details and a (free!) copy of the *Newlands Post*, edited by Patrick Hoyte with the assistance of David Beeby. This is an entirely junior society which was formed in April 1953, with seven members and is now twenty strong. The twenty-page *Post* is neatly printed (on a duplicator) and stapled, and there is a complete account of the society's philatelic adventures of 1956—displays, competitions, auctions, a visit to Congress at Brighton, and to the Tunbridge Wells Post Office, and a printing works. One of the highlights was a visit to London and a "Magic" shop (apparently not "391"?). For those thirsting for knowledge (or anxious to display it) the magazine has an article by Master Phillips on G.B. Constant Varieties, an ingenious Quiz and a Crossword. There is a hard-hitting President's Report, and some fascinating Club Notes from which I quote: "Members are advised NOT to bring cycles to meetings, and if any member is found letting tyres down he will be fined 1d. per tyre, the fine being divided between the Club and the owner. He will also have to pump up the tyres."

"Young Collector"

Well done, boys and girls of Newlands Road. You must get lots of fun out of your annual subscription of one shilling. Why not buy a Club bicycle-pump out of your credit balance of £4 13s. 5½d.?

One of our earliest reports in the Weekly Kent & Sussex Courier, Oct 1957.

CLUB'S CENTENARY

THE 100th meeting of the Newlands Road Philatelic Society, Tunbridge Wells, was held on Saturday when competition prizes were presented by Mr. Wilfrid B. Haworth.

Winners of the silver trophy — the Newlands Stamp—were David Reich and Patrick Hoyte, who tied for first place in the class for over 12½ year olds.

Third in the same class was Colin Fowle and fourth was David Beeboy. Under 12½ years winners were: 1 Christopher Bayly, 2 Peter Powell, 3 Bronwen Phillips, 4 Simon Timmis.

Two extra prizes were given by Mr. J. C. Cartwright, president of the Tunbridge Wells Philatelic Society. One for most improvement was won by Malcolm Clift and another for most promise in new members by John Botten.

Mr. Haworth, editor of "Stamp Collectors' Fortnightly" and secretary of the Melville Memorial Sub-committee of the Philatic Congress of Great Britain, spoke on "Taking a stamp to pieces."

Judges of the competition were Mr. J. C. Cartwright, Mr. J. A. Williams, Mr. Beever, Mr. C. Wells and Mr. D. Read.

Once we got a foothold in these three publications, they all regularly published reports of our meetings. On the next few pages are a sample of the many more that we had from these three, and after those there will be a few of the other accounts, including one Italian stamp magazine, and one UK National newspaper.

November 1956

Newlands Road P.S. By rights I ought to have been in Tunbridge Wells at the beginning of October, to present the prizes in the Society's competition and talk about the Melville Memorial Competition for Juniors. However, the doctors having got me by the leg, I could not make it. This go-ahead Junior Club in Tunbridge Wells, divides its competition into two sections, the over and the under twelves. This year there were sixteen entries out of a total of twenty-two members, a percentage which should make many senior societies blush with shame.

The Judges. Of these five were appointed, Miss H. N. Brett, Messrs. J. C. Cartwright, Brewer, Williams and Yardley, the last being a non-collector and the others very well-known philatelists. They were given the following scale of marks.

Philatelic Knowledge	...		20%
Mounting	...	... ...	20%
Arrangement	...	...	15%
Write-up	...	... ...	15%
Condition	...	... ...	10%
Originality	...	... ...	10%

In addition the non-collector judge was allowed 20% for interest with consequent reduction in the other points, and there was an over all allowance of 8% for age.

Starting with the Stamp Collectors Fortnightly, Edited by Wilfrid B Haworth

The Results. Colin Fowle, the Society's President, and Christopher Phillips, Hon. Secretary, also send me the results of the competition. In the Senior Section the boys have it all their own way: 1, Patrick Hoyle; 2, Colin Fowle; 3, David Reich; 4, Brian Clews. But in the Juniors, while the 1st prize went to Peter Lewis, the second and third were awarded to Bronwyn Lloyd Roberts and Susan Smith. His Worship the Mayor of Tunbridge Wells presented the prizes on October 13th.

Why? Now perhaps you may be wondering why I have given all these details. The answer is simple: my intention is to let you see what an enthusiastic junior society can do, when it really gets going. And you may as well know that the Newlands Road Society is only one of the Junior Clubs in Tunbridge Wells, (I suspect largely owing to the work of Mr. J. C. Cartwright and his helpers). Just study over the details I have given and I am sure that you will find several helpful points.

26th Oct 1957.

Newlands Road Philatelic Society. Thanks to the kind hospitality of Mr. and Mrs. Phillips, we were enabled to stay overnight with them so as to be available for the hundredth meeting of the Newlands Road Philatelic Society. This is a fine record for a society consisting solely of juniors and officered entirely by juniors: Christopher Phillips, the Hon. Secretary and Treasurer is to be warmly congratulated on the hard work he has put into organisation and running of the Society.

Stamp Collectors Fortnightly 26th Oct 1957.

The Newlands Stamp. The 100th meeting was the occasion of a new type of Annual Competition Award. Instead of the usual cup or shield the Society has had a silver plate of suitable size perforated round the four edges. This is mounted on an oak base and is suitably inscribed "The Newlands Stamp," and the date and details of the inauguration of the award. At the Societies' competition the five judges, Messrs. Cartwright, Reed, Paremer, Williams, all well-known philatelists, and Mr. C. Wells (hon. philatelist), decided that two entries tied for first place, namely those put in by Patrick Hoyle and David Reich, both in the Senior Class. Accordingly for the first year the trophy will carry the names of two joint winners.

* * * * *

Sadly, Wilfrid B Haworth died not long after he visited our club in 1957 as our guest speaker at our 100th meeting, and Stamp Collectors Fortnightly ceased publication. He was remembered for a time by the Philatelic Congress of Great Britain, and the World Association Of Young Stamp Collectors, who had awards and competitions in his memory.

WHY NOT . . .

"... erect a statue to Sir Rowland Hill? After all, Cromwell was celebrated for cutting off the head of a bad King, so why not honour Sir Rowland Hill for sticking on the head of a good Queen?"

From the "Newlands Post", Jan. 1959.

Incidentally, on January 2nd we welcomed ten members of the Newlands Road (Junior) Philatelic Society of Tunbridge Wells to "391" where "Mentor" lived up to his name and showed them pretty well all they wanted to see—stamp stock and strongrooms, magazine and catalogue editorial departments. And, but for the strongest persuasion, they would be in the "New Issues" office still!

Next section has a sample of the Gibbon's Stamp Monthly cuttings

Gibbons March 1958.

"SECRETARY'S NIGHTMARE"

Extracts from the "seconds" of the 1984th Meeting of the Newlands Road Philatelic Society, held one day in September, 1959, at 2.30 p.m.—

"At precisely 2.35 p.m. the first member arrived in muddy boots and torn clothes, and walked through the house leaving his mark for everyone to see. His excuse? 'I tripped over a matchstick when I saw a 3d. stamp in the road and I fell into some brambles.' Five minutes later hoards (sic) of members pushed their way thro' the doors . . . and windows. The Secretary spoke but was not heard, possibly because P–t–r Cl–ft and M–lc–lm P–w–ll were sitting next to each other, and someone shouted 'You give me the Pip'. After about 15 minutes the 'seconds' of the last meeting were read but not heard; the 1983rd Meeting only lasted 50 seconds. Reason? P–t–r Cl–ft and M–lc–lm P–w–ll had let down everyone's tyres, but luckily they were wearing pumps.

"The next business was an auction sale. 1st lot: a set of D– –tsch R– –ch inflationary stamps, no bid. 2nd lot: Silence. This continued until the 50th lot (the last) which was sold by and to the auctioneer, P–tr–ck H–yt–, for ½d. The thing that was so attractive about these stamps was that the lot had been put in by P–t–r V–n–s. The reason why so few lots were sold was afterwards assumed to be because of the presence of the 'Fairy Queen' (J–hn B–tt–n) who had cast a spell on all members except herself and the auctioneer because she wanted the V–n–s stamps, but the auctioneer beat her to it. Even the roaring of B– –by (Ly–n) was silenced". *From the "Newlands Post" January 1958 issue, published by the Newlands Road (Junior) Philatelic Society of Tunbridge Wells.*

Gibbons July 1958.

NEWLANDS AGAIN

More news from go-ahead Christopher Phillips, Secretary of the Newlands Road Philatelic Society who recently put on a good show at the Tunbridge Wells Hobbies Exhibition. The display included the four main printing processes, perforations, papers and inks, all illustrated by drawings and stamps. Also on show was a typed history of the Society, clippings of press reports of Society affairs, and a selection of books from their library. They got a B.B.C. "mention" and a lot of local publicity for their efforts. On April 15th the Society held its fifth anniversary birthday party in a hired room, and even the birthday cake was in the shape of a stamp! No doubt it was well perforated before the evening was over. Congratulations, Christopher. By the way, the Newlands Road boys have had some nice covers printed for the British Empire Games this month available at 4d. each, or they will post them to you bearing the complete set of Games stamps (3d., 6d., 1s. 3d.) at Cardiff on July 18th for 2s. 9d., stiffeners 2d. extra per cover. Write and remit quickly to Christopher Phillips, 15 Newlands Road, Tunbridge Wells.

The above report is the one which made our sales of the British Empire Games FDCs so successful. We sold nearly all the 1000 envelopes we had printed, and I posted over 300 in Cardiff.

Gibbons July 1959.

REGIONAL POLL

Young Peter Powell of the Newlands Road Philatelic Society, Tunbridge Wells, has given me the results of a poll held at the recent Hobbies Exhibition to find, in the opinion of visitors, the best-designed Regional stamp. Of the 80 votes, the Scotland 1s. 3d. won 34, Guernsey 3d., 15 and Jersey 3d., 7. All the rest had 5 or under, N. Ireland 6d. had one vote, Wales 1s. 3d., none! There must be some loyal Scots in Tunbridge Wells, Peter!

For Juniors of All Ages

By "MENTOR"

STARTING A CLUB (1)

I AM frequently asked by keen young stamp collectors how they can become members of a stamp club or, what is perhaps more interesting and important, how they can *start* a stamp club in their own district, either at school or in their own homes. Now Christopher Phillips, founder of the go-ahead Newlands Road Philatelic Society of Tunbridge Wells has come forward with some useful notes on the subject, intended for those keen young philatelists between the ages of, say, twelve and fifteen, boys or girls.

"If you know that some of your friends in your road, district or school, are stamp collectors you can have endless fun and, at the same time, learn the real values of stamps, by forming a stamp club. After getting together at a preliminary meeting you should first elect a President (to keep order, etc.), and a Secretary (to record the minutes and arrange meeting-places, displays, etc.). Both officers should be keen collectors and well-liked by everyone. Neither should attempt to "boss" the others but should help all members, even the less popular ones, and if arguments arise between them, peace should be restored in a firm, tactful manner. Officers should not take "sides" but might, in a quiet corner after the meeting, try to explain to the one who is wrong *why* he is wrong. Be helpful always."

Young Stamp Collectors.

Christopher says that once the Club gets going more officers will be necessary—Treasurer, Auctioneer, Librarian and maybe an Editor for your own magazine. But don't try to have too many officers to commence with; you will only get in a muddle!

"Subscriptions, if any, should be small. I think it is better to begin without any subscription at all until the Club is fairly well established. I have tried both methods. I started a 'Magic Circle' with a low subscription but after a few weeks it closed down through lack of support. The stamp club, now the Newlands Road Philatelic Society, had no subscription for the first three years, then it was voted to have an annual subscription of 1s. New clubs have little to offer their members in the early stages but you may well ask how the club got any money. Well, this was done by various means: buying and selling stamps, and auctions."

Next month we will see just how the Newlands Road boys and girls raised funds for their club, also how meetings are arranged and how interest is maintained year after year.

This was a two part series about how to start and run an ALL JUNIOR stamp club, published in Gibbons Stamp Monthly, May 1959 & June 1959.

Weald Monthly Dec 1960

NEWLANDS ROAD
PHILATELIC SOCIETY

Secretary:
PETER POWELL
39 Newlands Road, Tunbridge Wells

December Programme:

3—Auction Sale at 6 p.m. at Culverden House.

10—Speaker: Cyril Harmer, of the famous London Auctioneers Firm.

30—Visit to Brown Knight and Truscot Printing Works, Tonbridge at 2.30 p.m.

For Juniors of All Ages

By "MENTOR"

STARTING A CLUB (II)

LAST month in these columns I published a few hints from Christopher Phillips of the Newlands Road Philatelic Society, Tunbridge Wells, on starting a stamp club of your own, either at school or in your own district. It was his view that a subscription should not be levied at first until the club really gets going. But some funds are necessary to cover various odd items of expenditure, possibly for stationery or a small rental for the hire of a meeting-room, postages incurred in circulating club notices to members, etc. The Newlands Road boys and girls raised funds in a very practical way by holding auction sales of stamps, taking a small commission, about 2d. in the 1s., on all lots sold.

"Later on," says Christopher, "we bought large packets of stamps and resold them in several lots. We quite often made a good profit on 2s. 6d. and 5s. packets. Members also contributed their duplicates for sale in the auctions, all adding to the club funds." Club meetings should be arranged, or at least suggested by the members themselves with the Secretary actually conducting the correspondence and attending to the details for visiting speakers, or club visits to places of philatelic interest, such as exhibitions and other societies. The auction sale and stamp-swapping sessions are very popular features of club meetings and the season's programme should include several of these. Quiz competitions and talks by members should be arranged with caution; both can become boring unless they are well staged, and the member talks well and has an interesting collection. "These two kinds of meeting would go best at a school club where there is usually a master in charge. If you can get an adult to give a display all the better, but even this can get out of hand as the speaker knows so much and the members so little." (But it's a chance to *learn*, Christopher!).

He means, of course, that an adult talk and display should not be "above the heads" of the junior audience, and I am sure there must be many senior philatelists in the various long-established philatelic societies all over the country who would be willing and able to visit a keen and enthusiastic junior stamp club and show them some interesting stamps or a part of their collection, if application was made to the Society secretaries. Members themselves can show off their collections in club competitions, says Christopher. "Those who own loose-leaf albums should arrange their collections neatly and do a bit of writing-up; those with fixed-leaf albums have to enter the whole album. The judge should be a non-member, preferably an adult collector, and prizes (out of club funds) should be given for the best entries, with a small consolation prize for every entrant (this brings 'em in!). "Lastly, members who want correspondents abroad should join the "World Association of Young Stamp Collectors" whose President is Mr. Wilfred Haworth, the well-known philatelist and editor. The life subscription for clubs is only 10s., and their monthly "News Letter" is only 6s. 6d. per annum extra. The Honorary Secretary is: Mr. H. E. Pearse, 59, York Street, Twickenham, Middlesex.

The concluding part of the two part article in Gibbon's Stamp Monthly June 1959.

Kent & Sussex Courier and the Tunbridge Wells Advertiser, August 1958

SPOTLIGHT ON YOUTH

STARTED A STAMP COLLECTORS' CLUB

FIVE years ago a handful of boys, fired by a common affinity for stamps, decided to form their own philatelic society. After the early growing pains subsided, membership figures soared. Recently they were singled out for special mention on the B.B.C. programme "Town and Country."

Today the Newlands Road Philatelic Society is well known in the town, with a total strength of over 50 boys and girls—all under the age of 19. One of the founder members, and secretary, is 19-year-old Christopher Phillips, of 15, Newlands Road, Tunbridge Wells—the home of the society.

By sheer hard work and initiative, Christopher has put his society firmly on the map. Well-known philatelists have visited his home on club nights to give lectures, and Stanley Gibbons Magazine has outlined the club's history in a special feature.

"FOREIGN" MEMBERS

This publicity has widened the scope and attracted three "foreign" postal members—one from Grimsby, one from France, and another from Australia.

Although still jealously retaining their independence, they are now affiliated to the British Philatelic Association and the World Association of Young Collectors, and work closely with the Tunbridge Wells Society.

One of Christopher's latest ventures was a trip to the Empire and Commonwealth Games at Cardiff. He bought a whole series of stamps specially issued for the games in London, travelled down to Cardiff, spent the entire day sticking stamps on envelopes designed by the Newlands Society—and then posted them off to over 900 philatelists.

£14 PROFIT

This marathon effort realised a profit of £14 for the society!

Christopher left Skinners' School recently where he specialised in mathematics and science. Now that the society is firmly on its feet he plans to resign and go to college.

TOP SOCIALIST'S PLEDGE TO STAMP ENTHUSIASTS

NEWLANDS ROAD Philatelic Society—which consists entirely of young Tunbridge Wells stamp enthusiasts—has been conducting a vigorous campaign for pictorial postage stamps.

They have written to the Prime Minister, the Postmaster General, Mr. Jo Grimond, Mr. Richard Hornby and Mr. Harold Wilson asking if stamps depicting British beauty spots could be substituted for the conventional Queen's head stamps.

The letters to Mr. Macmillan and Mr. Grimond brought only formal acknowledgements. The petition to the Postmaster General brought a long explanation pointing out the "simple dignity" of the present stamps.

Mr. Hornby, the Tonbridge Division M.P., replied that he had no strong feelings on the subject, and later a second letter from the G.P.O., again explaining the reasons for not changing current issues.

EX-MINISTER'S SUPPORT

Mr. Harold Wilson's reply was different. He pledged his support to the campaign, reminding the young collectors that Mr. Ness Edwards, himself a former P.M.G. had pressed the same sugg[estion] from the opposition front b[ench].

"I shall be very glad to pass your letter on to him, since he is the Labour Party's official spokesman on post office affairs," said Mr. Wilson.

So it looks as if there is hope for the Newlands Road philatelists yet —especially if the Socialists can confound the public opinion polls and win the next election.

Kent & Sussex Courier 1959

Kent & Sussex Courier, 22nd April 1960

The three stamps of success

THE achievements of the Newlands Road Philatelic Society during the year included having a question asked in the House of Commons, an article in a Sunday newspaper, and taking a prominent part in the campaign for pictorial stamps for Britain.

Speaking at the seventh anniversary party of the society — members range in age from nine to 20—at Culverden House on Saturday afternoon, the past president, Christopher Phillips, said that future plans included further campaigning for pictorials and a display at this year's hobbies exhibition.

Past speakers included Mr. James Watson, assistant editor of Gibbons Stamp Monthly, and Mr. Marcus Samuel, a well-known stamp auctioneer.

David Reich, the new editor of the society's own magazine, the Newlands Post, urged members for more contributions. The librarian, 11-year-old Margaret Collier, appealed to the over-20 people present to use the library facilities more.

Officers elected were: president, Patrick Hoyte; secretary, Peter Powell; treasurer, Patrick Hoyte; librarian, Margaret Collier; vice-presidents, David Beeby and Christopher Selmes; assistant secretary, Simon Levett; editor, David Reich; auctioneer, Peter Veness; committee, Bronwen Phillips, Susan Smith, Peter Veness.

Kent & Sussex Courier, 24th Feb 1961

When Newlands Road Philatelic Society met on Saturday at Culverden House, Mr. Ian T. Hamilton gave a talk and display on "How a stamp is produced." He spoke of all the methods of printing stamps, starting with the line-engraved penny black and finishing with photogravure stamps, together with examples of each type of printing. His talk was illustrated with various excellent models and diagrams. Mr. Hamilton was thanked by Christopher Phillips.

Young stamp collectors are praised

Kent & Sussex Courier, Oct 1961

MR. CYRIL HARMER, of Harmer's, the London stamp auctioneers, presented the prizes at Newlands Road Philatelic Society prize-giving held at Culverden House, Tunbridge Wells, on Saturday.

Mr. Harmer spoke about his unique collection of Newfoundland airmail stamps. The stamps were displayed with a collection of photographs of the pioneers who made the first Atlantic crossing by air.

Mr. Harmer said he was impressed by the layout and arrangement of the stamps displayed by the young collectors, whose average age is 13 years. Patrick Smith won the trophy for gaining the highest marks in the competition. A stamp designing contest was won by Bronwen Phillips with a stamp to commemorate the Boy Scouts and Girl Guides Association.

SOCIETY NEARS ANNIVERSARY

Philatelists prepare to celebrate

A UNIQUE Tunbridge Wells society will be ten years old next April. It is the Newlands Road Philatelic Society, entirely independent, run by and for the benefit of the 10-21 age group.

The society owes its name to the fact that it was formed by four boys living in Newlands Road, Tunbridge Wells. It has 31 members, and is limited to 50 by its affiliation to the British Philatelic Association and two other national bodies.

Susan Smith, 15-year-old secretary of the society said that they met fortnightly; every second meeting was followed by a social evening.

"We have a competition each year, for the Newlands Shield," said Susan. "Everybody can enter six sheets of stamps."

She said they tried to get someone well-known in the stamp world in London, to address them occasionally.

Two help

They produce their own news-sheet, the "Newlands Post," twice a year, and have had a stand for several successive years at the Tunbridge Wells Hobbies Exhibition.

Two men who have helped the society are Mr. J. C. Cartwright, president of Tunbridge Wells Philatelic Society, and Mr. D. Read, owner of the Stamp Shop in Mount Sion.

President of the society is Peter Powell, and editor of the duplicated "Post" is David Reich.

Members plan full-scale celebrations to mark their society's anniversary next year.

Kent & Sussex Courier,
28th Sept 1962

Philatelists plan an exhibition

NEWLANDS Road Philatelic Society—the only all junior philatelic society in existence—is to hold an exhibition to celebrate its 10th anniversary.

The exhibition, which will be opened by the Mayor, Cr. John Spare, it is to be held at Tunbridge Wells Art Club premises in the Pantiles on Saturday, July 20.

Entry will be free and the exhibition will include members' displays, competitions and film shows.

Members' "swops" will be on sale with copies of the special issue of "Newlands Post," the society's magazine and souvenir covers.

Kent & Sussex Courier, June 21st 1963

Exhibition marks tenth anniversary

THE only all-junior philatelic society in existence—the Newlands Road Society, Tunbridge Wells, celebrated its tenth anniversary on Saturday by holding a stamp exhibition at the Art Club, in the Pantiles.

The Mayor of Tunbridge Wells, Cr. John Spare opened the exhibition which included a display of rare stamps lent to the society by the Stamp Collectors Promotion Council. The Tunbridge Wells society gave a number of stamps to be sold, and also helped towards the cost of the exhibition.

Visitors who wanted to help the society in its campaign for pictorial stamps signed a petition, which will be presented later to the Postmaster General. A film showing how stamps were printed was given by Harrison and Sons, of High Wycombe.

In our picture president of the Society, Peter Powell, points out a special stamp to the joint secretaries, Shirley Barr and Lynda Bringloe.

Kent & Sussex Courier, 26th July 1963 And the Advertiser

Also reported on The BBC SE Radio News

Other press cuttings A) Boys Own Paper

Jan 1959

★★★★★★★★

STAR LETTER

First Day Covers

Our local all-junior Stamp Club, the Newlands Road Philatelic Society, issued our own First Day Cover for the British Empire Games, held in Cardiff. We had 1000 special envelopes printed and, as a result of advertisements in prominent philatelic magazines, all but sixty-three were sold. Our Society made a profit of £14, a welcome addition to our funds. We also issued First Day Covers for the Boy Scout World Jamboree at Sutton Coldfield. We have over fifty members, some of them from overseas, and produce our own magazine. Earlier this year we celebrated our fifth birthday and we were mentioned in the B.B.C's *Town and Country* programme.

Patrick Hoyte, 15 Hon. Vice-President and Editor (Tunbridge Wells, Kent)

April 1959

NEWLANDS POST

An interesting stamp journal is being published by boys of the Newlands Road Philatelic Society. The journal consists of 12 foolscap pages, nicely produced on a duplicator, and containing articles, notes, book reviews, a list of members and their interests, advertisements and even an illustration! There is one amusing article by the journal's "printer" on how he went, with £62 in his pocket, to Charing Cross Post Office to buy over 2000 of the British Empire and Commonwealth Games stamps for affixing to first day covers. Other features of this issue of the journal are a philatelic crossword puzzle and a competition. The boys who run *Newlands Post*, as the journal is called, are pupils of Skinners' School, but members are welcome from any part of the country, and membership is open to girls as well. Details can be obtained from the Hon. Secretary, Peter Powell, 39 Newlands Road, Tunbridge Wells, Kent. *Details of this go-ahead club appeared in January* POST—*Ed.*

National "Children's Newspaper"

April 11th

CELEBRATING its sixth birthday next week is the Newlands Road Philatelic Society, of Tunbridge Wells. At its first meeting the Society had seven members and its funds amounted to 4½d.

The honorary secretary, Peter Powell (pictured here), who attends the Skinners' School, tells me that the Society now has 48 members, almost all aged between nine and seventeen, and they have nearly £14 in the funds!

As well as holding fortnightly meetings, the Society arranges a philatelic display at the annual Tunbridge Wells Hobbies Exhibition and publishes its own magazine, The Newlands Post. The Society's next meeting, its 153rd, will, needless to say, be a birthday party. Many happy returns! C. W. HILL

March 19th

PATRICK HOYTE, who attends Tonbridge School, is the Editor of *Newlands Post*, the magazine of the Newlands Road Philatelic Society, of Tunbridge Wells. He has just sent me the latest number, the seventh, which contains an interesting assortment of news items, articles, and puzzles.

Stamps belonging to members of the Newlands Road Society will be displayed at the Tunbridge Wells Hobbies Exhibition, from 20th to 23rd April. Members, almost all of whom are under 18, will also be campaigning for "Pictorial Stamps for Britain!"

They believe that Great Britain ought to have low-value stamps which include a portrait of the Queen but also show views of famous buildings, historic monuments, and some of Britain's beautiful scenery. At present our only pictorial stamps are the high values, half-a-crown and upwards, which are double the normal size. Visitors to the Society's stand at the Hobbies Exhibition will be asked to vote "Yes" or "No" in a special poll. C. W. HILL.

March 1961

Children's Newspaper, 25 Mar 1961

AMONG my mail recently have been two interesting stamp club magazines. One, the News Letter of the World Association of Young Stamp Collectors, lists the prizewinners of the 1961 Wilfrid Haworth Memorial competition. The Association has members in many countries, so the monthly News Letter provides a useful means of keeping collectors in touch. The other magazine is the Newlands Post, containing an account of the 200th meeting of the Newlands Road Philatelic Society, of Tunbridge Wells.

This is a notable achievement, for almost all the members of the Society are under 18.

C. W. HILL

13th July 1963

Tenth Birthday of a Junior Stamp Club

A STAMP exhibition is being held on 20th July at the Art Club Rooms, The Pantiles, Tunbridge Wells. It celebrates the tenth anniversary of the Newlands Road Philatelic Society.

This is run entirely by junior collectors in Tunbridge Wells. David Green, Editor of the Society's magazine, says that the Society now has 30 members, the youngest being—appropriately—ten years old.

With compliments,

C. W. Hill,

2 Trysull Gardens,
Wolverhampton,
England.

Philatelic Magazine, Aug 12th 1960

Wilfred Haworth Memorial

THE Newlands Road Philatelic Society of Tunbridge Wells recently decided to establish a memorial to the late Wilfred Haworth, in the form of some periodically offered prize or trophy for junior collectors. Details are to be worked out later.

In the meantime, the Society is preparing to market a specially printed First Day Cover for the Great Britain Europa stamps due out on September 19th. Half the profits on the sales of this cover will be given to the Melville Memorial Sub Committee for the setting up of a Haworth Memorial Competition.

News of this is announced in the current issue of the Society's bulletin *Newlands Post*. Editor is Mr. David Reich, and he would be glad to hear from anyone interested in the scheme referred to above. His address is: 39, Newlands Road, Tunbridge Wells, Kent.

Philatelic Magazine, June 3td 1960

NEWLANDS ROAD.—During the Tunbridge Wells Hobbies Exhibition a poll for or against pictorial stamps was held. Result: For (335), Against (27). A petition for pictorials will be sent to the local Member of Parliament. At the Annual General Meeting the following officers were elected: President (Mr. P. Hoyte), Vice-Presidents (Messrs. D. Beeby and C. Selmes), Secretary (Mr. P. Powell), Asst. Secretary (Mr. S. Levett), Treasurer (Mr. P. Hoyte), Librarian (Miss M. Collier), Editor (Mr. D. Reich), Auctioneer (Mr. P. Veness), Committee Members (Mr. P. Veness, Miss S. Smith and Miss Bronwen Phillips).

NUMERO SPECIALE PER «SICILIA 59»

il COLLEZIONISTA

ITALIA FILATELICA

THE COLLECTOR'S INTERNATIONAL MAGAZINE

N. 10 Direttore: GIULIO BOLAFFI

Una delle più attive Società filateliche inglesi è la « Newlands Road Philatelic Society » di Tunbridge Wells, nel Kent. Essa ha appena celebrato il suo sesto anniversario; quando venne costituita, nel 1953, contava sette iscritti, ed il capitale sociale ammontava a quattro pence e mezzo. I suoi membri sono ora 48; la società organizza riunioni quindicinali oltre ad allestire ogni anno il padiglione filatelico alla « Hobbies Exhibition » di Tunbridge Wells. La Società pubblica anche una rivista, intitolata « The Newlands Post ». Sono realizzazioni di cui andrebbe fiera anche una società di antica costituzione; e che acquistano maggior rilievo se si pensa che i soci sono tutti ragazzi fra i 9 ed i 17 anni, e l'attivissimo segretario, Peter Powell, va ancora a scuola!

C. W. HILL

Philatelic Magazine, Feb 20th 1959

First day cover of the new Great Britain 4½d. stamp comes on a specially designed envelope from the Newlands Road Philatelic Society. The design emphasises that in 1892 a 4½d. stamp was the rate for 2 to 3 lb., while in 1959 it is for 1 to 2 oz.

NEWLANDS ROAD PHILATELIC SOCIETY

(Affiliated to P.C. of G.B. & W.A.Y.S.C.)

THE ONLY ALL JUNIOR SOCIETY

Your ref.
Our ref.

Please reply to :-

21) Affiliations etc

As the club grew and got stronger, it became even better by joining three national Organisations. The first we joined was the BPA (British Philatelic Association), mainly to find new possible speakers. We also came across the World Association of Young Stamp Collectors, run by an elderly disabled man, friends with Wilfrid B Haworth. “World” was a little grand, but it did have members in some foreign countries, and “Young” was young at Heart. But we got on with the owner and he gave us, after a while, free life membership; several of our members did get a few stamp collecting friends in other countries. One year Patrick Hoyte and I had a philatelic race of a letter round the

The World Association
of Young Stamp Collectors

THIS is to certify that

THE NEWLANDS ROAD PHIL^C SOC^TY.

is a Life Member of this Association.

Reg'd No. 394

Date 16. XI. 57

Hon. Secretary.

59, York Street, TWICKENHAM, Middlesex.

world, calling in at least 7 countries. Not only did my letter win, but sadly Patrick never saw his again.

This was on a folded card with instructions in-

side. Remember this was in 1958. Postage rates will have changed considerably, as will people's address. It was supposed to go by SURFACE mail; that is why it

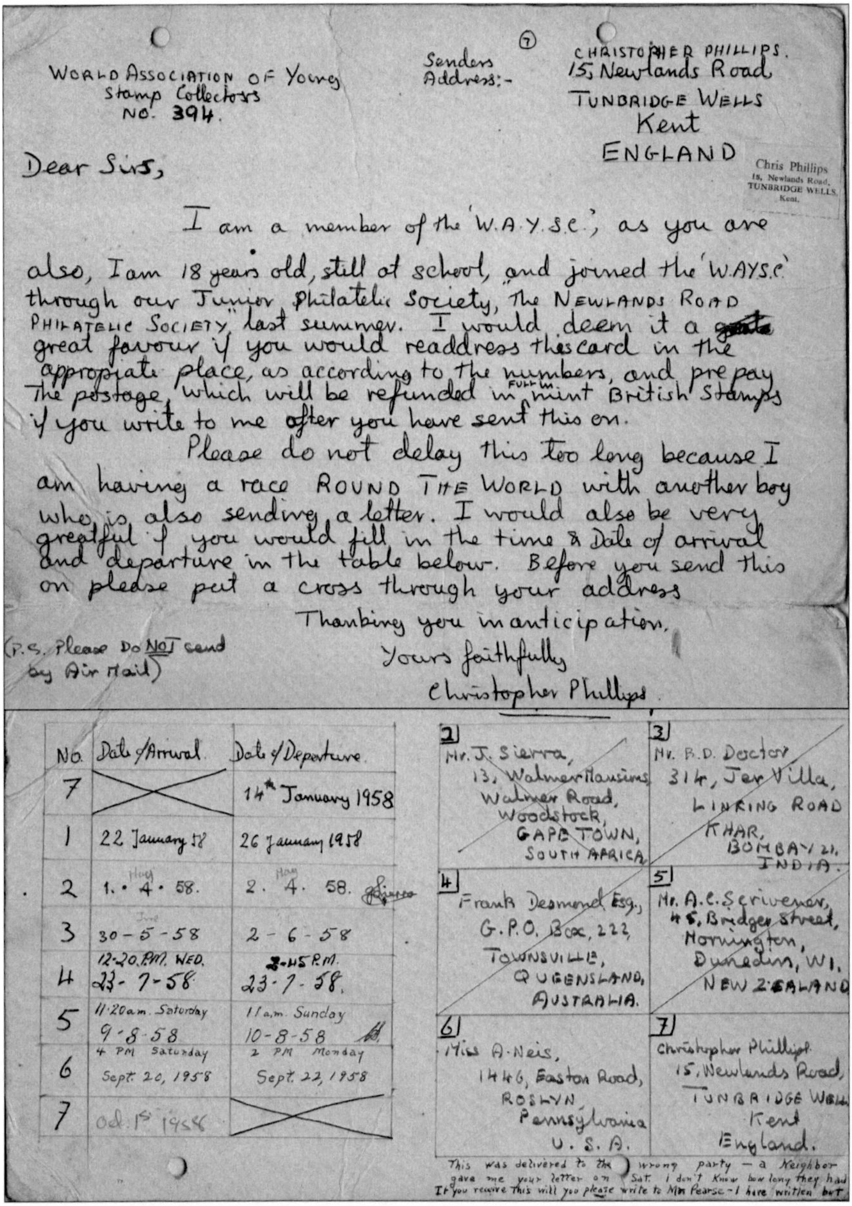

WORLD ASSOCIATION OF Young Stamp Collectors NO. 394.

Senders Address:- CHRISTOPHER PHILLIPS. 15, Newlands Road TUNBRIDGE WELLS Kent ENGLAND

Chris Phillips 15, Newlands Road, TUNBRIDGE WELLS, Kent.

Dear Sirs,

I am a member of the 'W.A.Y.S.C.', as you are also, I am 18 years old, still at school, and joined the 'W.AYS.C' through our Junior Philatelic Society, The NEWLANDS ROAD PHILATELIC SOCIETY, last summer. I would deem it a great favour if you would readdress this card in the appropiate place, as according to the numbers, and prepay the postage, which will be refunded in FULL in mint British Stamps if you write to me after you have sent this on.

Please do not delay this too long because I am having a race ROUND THE WORLD with another boy who is also sending a letter. I would also be very greatful if you would fill in the time & Date of arrival and departure in the table below. Before you send this on please put a cross through your address

Thanking you in anticipation,

Yours faithfully

Christopher Phillips.

(P.S. Please Do NOT send by Air Mail)

No.	Date of Arrival	Date of Departure
7	X	14th January 1958
1	22 January 58	26 January 1958
2	1. May 4. 58.	2. May 4. 58.
3	30 - 5 - 58 June	2 - 6 - 58
4	12-20 P.M. WED. 23 - 7 - 58	2-45 P.M. 23 - 7 - 58.
5	11·20 a.m. Saturday 9 - 8 - 58	11 a.m. Sunday 10 - 8 - 58
6	4 PM Saturday Sept. 20, 1958	2 PM Monday Sept. 22, 1958
7	Oct. 1st 1958	X

2) Mr. J. Sierra, 13, Walmer Mansions, Walmer Road, Woodstock, CAPE TOWN, SOUTH AFRICA

3) Mr. B.D. Doctor, 314, Jer Villa, LINKING ROAD KHAR, BOMBAY 21. INDIA.

4) Frank Desmond Esq., G.P.O. Box, 222, TOWNSVILLE, QUEENSLAND, AUSTRALIA.

5) Mr. A.C. Scrivener, 45, Bridger Street, Hornington, Dunedin, W1. NEW ZEALAND

6) Miss A. Neis, 1446, Easton Road, ROSLYN, Pennsylvania U.S.A.

7) Christopher Phillips. 15, Newlands Road, TUNBRIDGE WELLS Kent England.

This was delivered to the wrong party – a Neighbor gave me your letter on Sat. I don't know how long they had It you receive this will you please write to Mr Pearse – I have written but took so long. The WAYSC no longer exists.

The third main affiliation was to the Philatelic Congress of Great Britain, the group who organised the National Melville Competition. By joining this, we were then able to have two stabs at having entries sent up to the Melville competition. We were the only ALL junior club to be accepted, and the first ever Junior club. After we had joined some school clubs also joined.

I believe we joined the Kent Federation of Philatelic Societies as well.

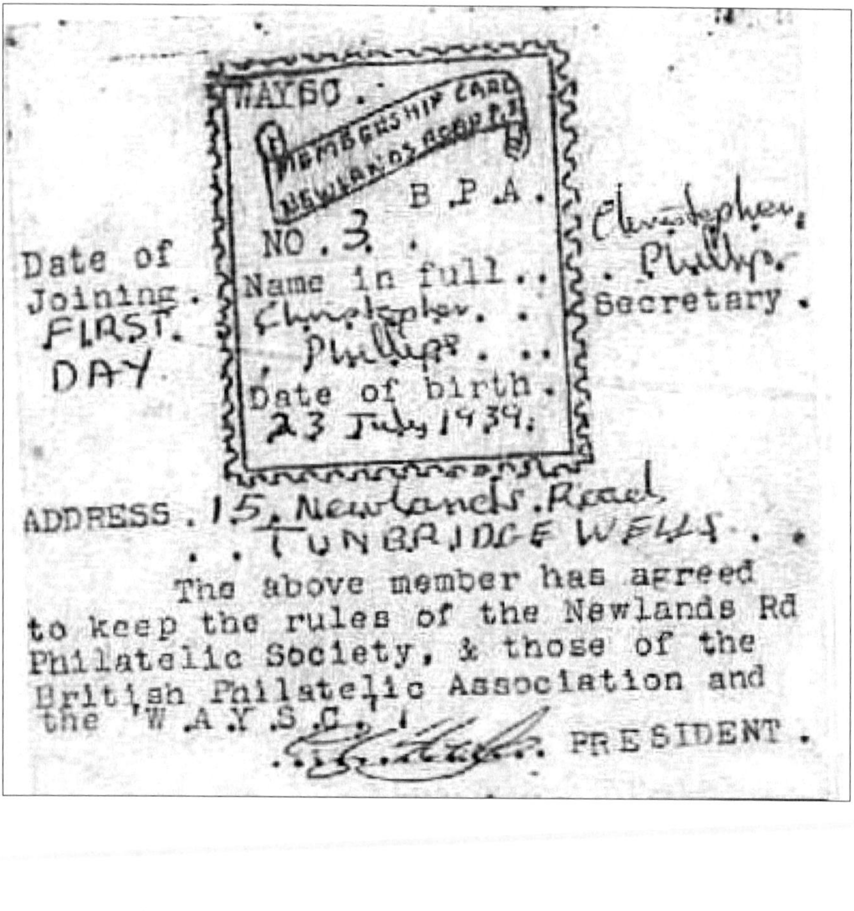

WAYSC.

MEMBERSHIP CARD NEWLANDS ROAD P.S.

B.P.A.

NO. 3.

Date of Joining. FIRST. DAY.

Name in full.. Christopher. Phillips...

Date of birth. 23 July 1939;

Christopher. Phillips. Secretary.

ADDRESS. 15, Newlands. Road, TUNBRIDGE WELLS..

The above member has agreed to keep the rules of the Newlands Rd Philatelic Society, & those of the British Philatelic Association and the 'W.A.Y.S.C.'

PRESIDENT.

22) 10th Anniversary 1963

Many clubs will last longer than 10 years, so not so good perhaps, but how often do clubs started, and always run, by youngsters under 21 last even 5 years? Yes, we had some adult help, but the vast majority was organised and run by under 21s. Proper records were kept of all meetings, we had our own newsletter, and ran our own First Day Cover service, which provided most of the finance. We had tours round Printing works, in Tunbridge Wells, Tonbridge and London. We saw the Post Office Sorting in action in Tunbridge Wells, we saw round the Editorial offices in Tunbridge Wells and London, we saw behind the scenes in the biggest Stamp company, Stanley Gibbons, and the Stamp Printers Offices Showrooms in London. So to have our own public exhibition in a very famous part of Tunbridge Wells (The Pantiles) was quite an achievement.

And who better to officially declare the exhibition open, than the Mayor of Tunbridge Wells? On the following pages are more photos at the exhibition.

From memory, the Tunbridge Wells Philatelic Society helped with the hiring of the room, where they normally had the weekly Wednesday night meetings.

In the "NEWLANDS POST" was a plan and a pro-

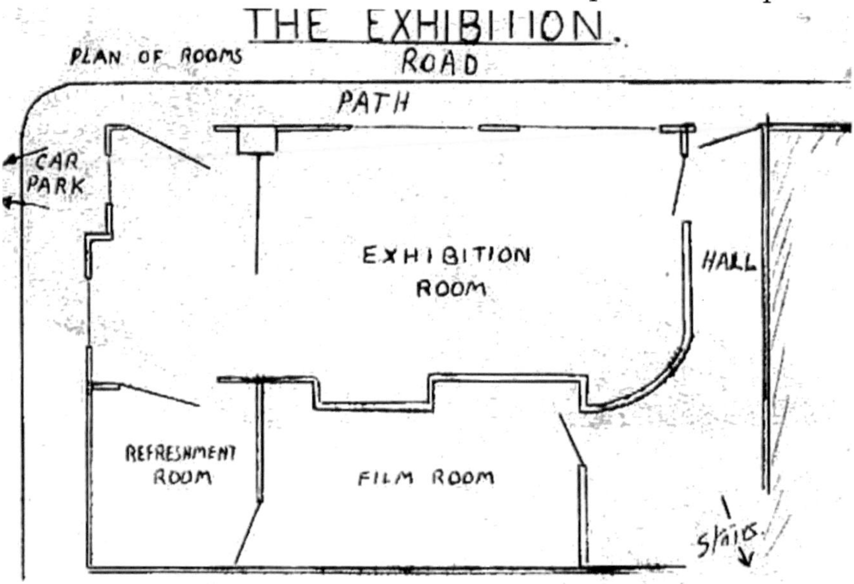

gramme. Apart from displays by several members, we had a display by the "Stamp Collecting Promotional Council", a section about our Campaign for Small Pictorial Postage Stamps, and a film, on loan from Harrison & Sons (the stamp printers) about printing stamps by the Photogravure method.

PROGRAMME.

10.00 am.	Doors Open.
10.30	Official Openning by Councillor John Spare, Mayor of Royal Tunbridge Wells.
10.45	Refreshments on sale.
11.15	First film showing (Printing of Photogravure stamps by Harrison & Sons Ltd.) (To be shown a regular intervals)
5.00 pm.	Results of competitions & draw.
6.00 pm.	Exhibition Closes. -oO Oo-

The entrance. The name was spelt out in damaged stamps.

Below: the welcoming and information desk.

David Green Shirley Burr (A visitor) Bronwen Phillips

Visitors and members inspecting the exhibits in the exhibition room

Another part of the exhibition room with visitors and members.

Lynda Bringloe presenting the Mayoress with flowers, after the official opening.

Peter Powell explaining about one of the stamps in the collection to his joint secretaries, Lynda Bringloe & Shirley Burr.

The main entrance again.

23) Main Members & Membership

Peter Powell Shirley Burr & Lynda Bringloe David Green

Bronwen Phillips Colin Fowle, David Reich, (Wilfrid B Haworth) Patrick Hoyte

The main organisers over the years (those in italics are pictured here):

Myself, Robin Grey, *Colin Fowle*, *Peter Powell, David Green, Shirley Burr, Lynda Bringloe*, John Teasdale, *Bronwen Phillips, David Reich, Patrick Hoyte*, David L-R, *Susan Smith,* Peter Veness, Robert Romer.

Susan Smith Me

Robin & Clive Grey

Andrew Crighton,
Mark Nicholson &
Graham Camfield

24) Death Of NRPS & Later Memories

Kent & Sussex Courier, Jan 15th 1965

ONLY ALL-JUNIOR STAMP CLUB FACES A CRISIS

School examinations stop the get-up-and-go youngsters

TUNBRIDGE WELLS is the home of a unique youth club—the Newlands Road Philatelic Society. There is no other all-junior society of stamp-collectors in the country.

Since its foundation nearly 12 years ago the society has been completely independent, paying its own way without difficulty.

Its present membership is some 25-30, but only about half-a-dozen of these are really active.

Now it is facing a crisis: all its leading members are working hard for their G.C.E. "O" and "A" level examinations, and so cannot give much time to organising the society's activities.

The acting president, 16-year-old Dave Green, of 69 Nursery Road, High Brooms, believes there must be many young people who would be eager to join if only they knew something about the society.

Young people, for example, who feel as he himself did when he joined just three years ago.

"I was already a stamp-collector," he said, "and was looking for a club. But the Tunbridge Wells club didn't appeal to me because it was an adult club."

The cost

Age-limits for members range from nine (or even younger) up to 20.

What does a new member need? Just an interest in stamps.

Like any other hobby, stamp-collecting can cost as little or as much as you like:

"You can spend as little as 5s. to 10s. to start," said Dave.

The Newlands Road Philatelic Society—so called because it was originally founded in Newlands Road—has a wide range of activities: talks, auctions, exhibitions, competitions, and film shows. It also prints its own first-day covers, and has its own magazine.

What they did

But its most striking activities have been outside Tunbridge Wells—it believes in trying hard to get things done, instead of just sitting back and moaning "Why don't they . . .? why can't they . . .?"

These are some of the things which members thought the G.P.O. should do: issue small, low-value pictorial stamps; issue better-designed and more imaginative commemorative stamps; publicise new issues of stamps well in advance; set up a Philatelic Bureau: reverse the date and slogan positioning of machine cancellations: make more use of pictorial slogan cancellations.

And this is what members did: they constantly wrote to the G.P.O. and the Postmaster-General; sent two petitions to Parliament; wrote to all Kent M.P.'s; wrote to Mr. Harold Macmillan (then Prime Minister), Mr. Grimond, Mr. Gaitskell and Mr. Wilson; and also conducted a public opinion poll.

Some young people may have a slight interest in stamps, but will ask: "Why should I join a club, and take this hobby more seriously? Anyway, what's in it for me?"

This may be a "wrong" question, but it deserves a fair answer.

The answer is simply that an interest in stamps can help people of all ages deepen their interest and understanding of other hobbies—history of railways, ships and the sea, sports, Scouts and Guides, history and great men, the arts, world peace, Red Cross, animals and even space travel.

● Young people who would like to join the Newlands Road Philatelic Society should get in touch with: Dave Green, 69 Nursery Road, High Brooms, Tunbridge Wells; or with Lynda Bringloe, 138 Powder Mill Lane, High Brooms, Tunbridge Wells.

A cover issued by the Newlands Road Philatelic Society

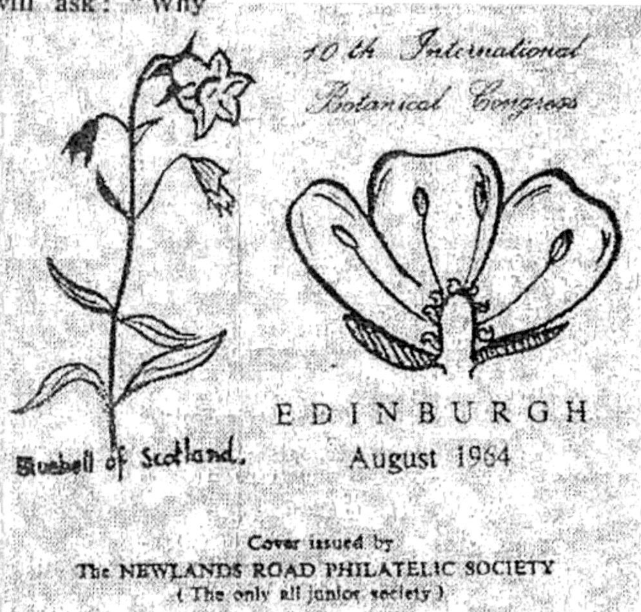

24) Death Of NRPS & later memories

After that big article (previous two pages) in the Kent and Sussex Courier, the club got back up again.

A new committee was elected at the 290th meeting on May 8th 1965. At the following meeting too few members attended to have a quorum, and the minutes then have a gap of over a year; the 292nd meeting was not until July 9th 1966. A copy of the actual minutes is on the following page.

Then crisis struck again, and a special meeting was called for July 30th 1966 at the Pantiles; the Tunbridge Wells PS funded this for the club.

Kent & Sussex Courier
July 15th 1966

Newlands Road Philatelic Society

SPECIAL MEETING

at

61 THE PANTILES
6 p.m. to 8 p.m.
SATURDAY, JULY 30th

DISPLAY OF STAMPS and SHOW OF SLIDES

New Members Welcome at this meeting

Kent & Sussex Courier
Summer 1965

New lease of life

NEWLANDS Road Philatelic Society, Tunbridge Wells, which has been in danger of disbanding because of lack of support, has gained a new lease of life.

At a special meeting on Saturday, a new committee was appointed comprising Mr. Robert Romer (chairman), Mr. Andrew Crighton (secretary), Mr. Graham Camfield, (treasurer), and Mr. Mark Nicholson (librarian).

The retiring president, Mr. David Green, said: "I am pleased that the 13 years taken to build up the society have not been wasted."

The meeting included an illustrated talk by a member, Mr. Christopher Phillips, who outlined the society's history. An auction raised over £2 for society funds.

The society is the only all-junior (under 21) philatelic group in Great Britain.

The minutes of the 292nd meeting of the Newlands Road Philatelic Society.

The meeting was held at 6.00. pm. on Saturday July 9th 1966 at 138 Powder Mill Lane.

It was decided, due to lack of support at this meeting, to hold one big meeting at the Art Club to determine whether to disband the Society, or whether to make a final effort to put the club on its feet depending on attendance.

The meeting closed at 7.15. pm. with 4 members, 1 honorary member, and 2 ~~members~~ visitors present.

signed:-
Lynda Bringloe
(Jt - Secretary)

The club started meeting again but was now meeting sometimes in Newlands, Langton Green, as then Andrew Crighton took on the organising of the club,

Kent & Sussex Courier,
July 15th 1966

CLUB'S STRUGGLE GOES ON

THE meeting last weekend to rekindle enthusiasm for Tunbridge Wells' unique junior stamp club—the Newlands Road Philatelic Society—attracted only about seven people. Another meeting to save the club is to be held in Tunbridge Wells on July 30—this time at a more central place, the Tunbridge Wells Art Club, 61 The Pantiles. It is hoped that a new committee will be elected.

Major awards

Mr. David Green, the president, will survey for newcomers the society's many achievements and there will be a slide-show and a stamp display by society members and members of its "big brother" society—Tunbridge Wells Philatelic Society.

Newlands Road P.S. is the only all junior (under 21) stamp club in Great Britain and possibly in the world.

It became known nationally because of its fight for pictorial stamps.

The club is also a member of the Philatelic Congress of Great Britain and members have won major awards.

THE NEW committee of the Newlands Philatelic Society, Tunbridge Wells, elected at a special meeting on Saturday are, from the left, Andrew Crighton, Mark Nicholson, Graham Camfield and David Green, who resigned from the chair, but will remain on the committee. Saturday's meeting brought a new lease of life for the society, which has been facing disbandment.

and he lived in Langton. They still had some meetings back in the Newlands Road region of Tunbridge Wells. But in spite of all this only a few members attended, and for about 4 meetings in a row there were not enough members present to hold a meeting for the lack of a quorum. And so, see the next page for the very last recorded minutes of this great little all junior stamp club.

Robert Romer reports "There were a few more meetings after that, there was definitely a meeting on 4 February. There were subsequent meetings (approximately monthly) until 22 July when no one turned up for a meeting at my home. Technically this could not be regarded as a meeting since I was on my own. On 9 September there was an attempt to recruit new members at the Langton Green fete where NRPS had a stall. This was unsuccessful and so marked the end of the stamp club."

The last recorded meeting.
SO SAD after so long, nearly 14 years.
This must be a record of any all junior club for lasting so long.

The Minutes of the 304th meeting of the Newlands Road Philatelic Society 1967

The meeting was held at 13, Newlands, Langton Green on Saturday January 4th at 6·00 pm.
the minutes of the last meeting were read and confirmed by Robert Romer, president.
There was an auction at which 4/6d was raised in 4 lots.
There was then a short discussion about future events in the society.
The meeting closed at 8·00 pm with 5 members and 4 visitors present.

[signature] (Hon Sec) R Romer (Hon. Pres.).

BUT I hope that this story will give encouragement for other juniors to run their own clubs.

The Newlands Stamp became part of the National Junior Competition awards, as the "School's Trophy". It is awarded each year to the best set of entries by a school in the annual national Junior Competition. The first time it was awarded was at the London International Stamp Exhibition in 1980, to the School Stamp Club that I was running at the time!

Then 5 years later The Newlands Stamp was awarded to the

next school stamp club that I ran at the Claremont Fan Court School, Esher.

Then five years later, in Alexandra Palace, at the 1990 London International Stamp Exhibition, a whole series of display boards was erected all about The Newlands Road Philatelic Society. I also have given a few talks to societies about the club (and am willing to do more!)

In 2003 I produced a set of four "SMILERS" stamps to celebrate the 50th Anniversary of its founding. There were four different labels, and a cover, and also a cachet. When I was arranging for some covers to be posted in Tunbridge Wells on the 50th Anniversary (15th April 2003), the man in charge at the local Post Office said as I had a cachet made, why did I not cancel the stamps with that, and he then agreed to use the Tunbridge Wells "Skeleton" handstamp as proof of posting. I found out, AFTERWARDS, that this should not have happened. The use of "Smilers" for a stamp club was almost certainly the first time that had happened. Only one complete Smilers sheet was made of each design, and about half were used on FDCs. I have the majority of

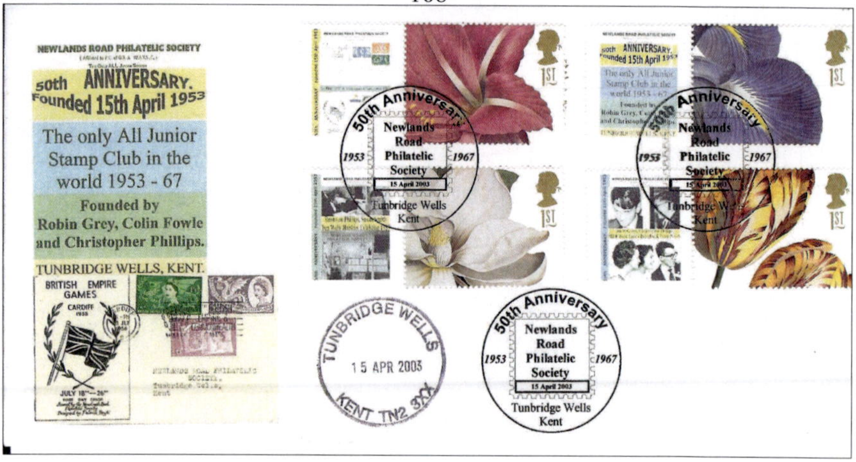

the rest in mint condition.

The four designs of the labels attached to the real stamps used on the "Smilers" stamps. They show:

1) The basic facts

2) The first FDC & the 10th Anniversary Cover

3) 5 of the main organisers {David Green; Myself; Shirley Burr; Lynda Bringlow; & Peter Powell}

4) Two more {Bronwen Phillips & Susan Smith} and a T W Hobbies exhibition Photo.

Above, a half complete sheet of one design of the labels, and below, one example of each of each of the others.

A complete sheet had 20 1st Class stamps with 10 different floral stamps. The other half was identical to the above. So there were in fact 40 different possible combinations of stamps with our 4 labels. Nearly half were used on the covers, the rest in my collection.

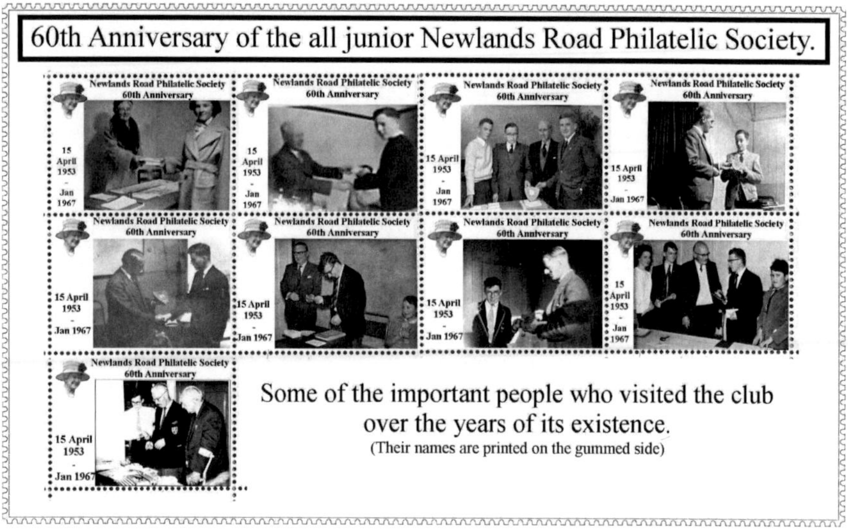

Ten years later, for the 60th anniversary, I had printed 5 different miniature sheets of stamp-like designs; these three were in B&W, showing some of the *famous* adult speakers who came to the club and some Newlands Posts, and press cuttings. These were all printed on gummed paper. No covers were made of these.

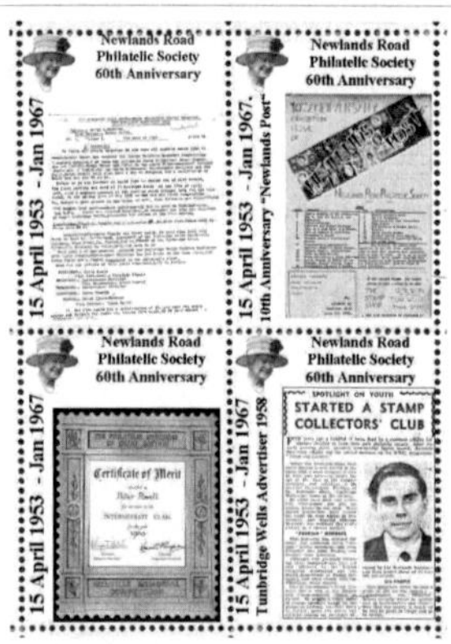

These four labels show the 1st Newlands Post (typewritten with carbon copies), the 10th Anniversary edition duplicated including colour on the front page, one of many certificates won by members, and a write-up in the local paper.

The greatest national publicity the club got was for its campaign for the Post Office to issue small low value pictorial postage stamps. Viscount Elibank had printed 100 copies of the designs by Charles Rang for us to use. We had questions asked in the House of Commons, and a news item in the Sunday Observer. Recently we discovered our campaign letters are now housed in the Postal History Museum.

60th Anniversary of the founding of the all junior

Newlands Road Philatelic Society.

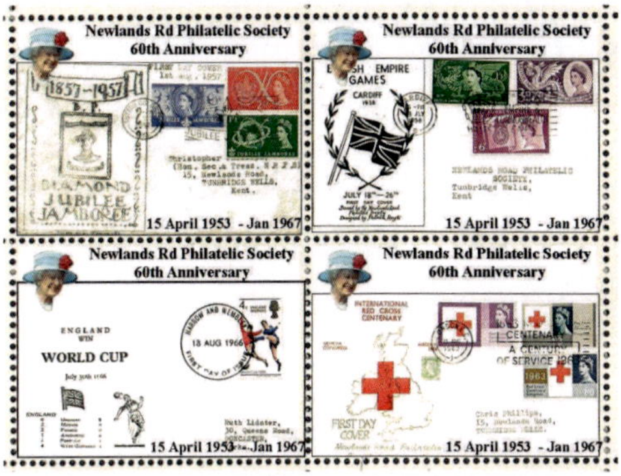

Funding was by subscription and fund raising by selling our own First Day Covers for British issues 1957 - 67.

The four covers illustrated all had special cancellations: Sutton Coldfield for the scouts, Cardiff for Empire Games, Wembley for World Cup and London for the Phosphor Red Cross set.

Only about 40 of each sheet were printed. The two colour sheets showed iconic FDCs. The first showed the Scouts, the Empire games, the England Winners Cover (1966) and the Red Cross FDCs. The second showed Peter Powell showing the joint secretaries round the 10th Anniversary Exhibition; the 10th Anniversary FDC; the minutes of the first ever meeting; and the 50th Anniversary Cover with the "Smilers" stamps.

The other way that the club will live on, in name, will be the fact that I will give talks to philatelic and other societies about how children can run their own clubs.

A few of these sheets are available for sale, from the author. At £1 per sheet, or all 5 for £4.50

60th Anniversary of the founding of the all junior

Newlands Road Philatelic Society.

These labels show the minutes of the first meeting, the 10th Anniversary public Exhibition, the souvenir cover of that exhibition and the 50th Anniversary Smilers FDC

25) 1962/3 Snow Palace Like Home

On the night of Dec 26th 1962 there fell from the sky, for 14 hours non-stop, billions upon billions of snowflakes, and not only was Tunbridge Wells completely covered in a foot deep white fluffy blanket of starry hexagons, but so was much of the UK. I remember noticing the snow falling at about 10 pm, and hoping it would be still falling when I woke up. I was not to be disappointed. Still falling, it was about 6 inches deep. I hurriedly ate up my Shredded Wheat, got dressed to go outside, and walked around the garden and the road, being awed by the stillness and the

whiteness. I remembered having had a dream, about 6 years before this event, when in the dream there was a flash, and then everything was covered in white, the tall fir trees opposite were drooping with the thick wads of snow and everywhere was WHITE!

The dream had suddenly come

true. I went back into the house and emerged with my camera (an Ilford Pronto), and managed to get my bike out of the garage, and proceeded to cycle through 6 inches of snow that was slightly crunchy. I had to walk up Newlands Rise, but nowhere else did I need to walk, and I cycled down to the Town Centre and took

several pictures of buses and cars attempting, unsuccessfully, to climb up Mount Pleasant. There was a salt lorry with two men on the back shovelling salt

onto the road - none of those machines in those days, all down to man-power. There was little traffic about at all, but there were a few brave cars and lorries and the very occasional bus. Eventually I returned to Newlands Road, to find my sister and her friend Jane trying to roll a **huge** snowball on what was the grass verge outside no 13. So I was asked to help. The snow by now was about 10 inches deep. So as the ball rolled towards our house at no 15 it quite quickly got bigger. We stopped at our gate (still on the grass verge) and now it was nearly as tall as myself. What does one do with a large snowball?

Well, it was dinner time, so we went in and had lunch as quickly as possible, hoping the snow would continue, though it was slowing down now. When we went out again, we made the decision to turn the snowball into an igloo. So we carved out parts and made the bits into snow bricks, and then using Dad's wheelbarrow we made many more snow bricks. Gradually the igloo took shape, the sides curving inwards, until we were left with a hole at the top. Again using the wheelbarrow, we made one large "brick" to

cover the hole in the roof, and lo and behold we had an igloo! The entrance was about half my height so we had to crawl inside. So far we had no tunnel, but there was a rudimentary door facing due North! We had left a rectangular kitchen baking tin with water in outside, whilst we were building, and I cut a rectangular hole for a window in the south facing wall. I took the picture of Bronwen, Jane and a baby Anne through the window. Then we carefully took the thin ice sheet off the top of the water in the tin, and placed it in the hole. Now we had natural glass window. By now it was getting dark, and we had tea. After tea we took my small battery driven tape recorder and a candle tin to the igloo and spent a little time there listening to the latest pop music. It was surprising how warm it felt inside. It froze up again overnight, and I decided to pin a message on the outside of the igloo: "SOLVE THE HOUSING PROBLEM - BUILD AN IGLOO". Also we added, "Please put money in the box for the Freedom From Hunger Campaign."

It was during this cold spell that I went for my in-

terview to go to Swansea University for the year course for Teacher Training. After the interview I walked on the frozen sea before returning home, and of course took a photo of the sea ice on the beach. There was not even a hint of snow there, but it was VERY VERY COLD; the boating lake that we been boating on only last summer was now a ice rink, with about a foot of ice. This may not seem relevant to this book's story, but I will connect it up shortly.

On the Sunday there was an overnight blizzard, and the next day was when we finished off the curved tunnel to the entrance. That Sunday my father and I walked to Meeting (Religious Society Of Friends, Quakers) along the main road, as the footpaths were almost impossible to walk along, and the road had less deep snow on it, and no cars or buses seemed to be running! On the Tuesday night we had a small group of Young Quakers round to see in the new year, and a couple of other friends.

At 11.45 pm on the last day of 1962, we all went inside the igloo, took a photo, listened to pop music on my tape recorder in candle light, and next year we came out and took another photo. Yes, the igloo was large enough to accommodate 7 of us, JUST.

The next Friday there was a photo in the Kent & Sussex Courier. Gradually, as the winter wore on and on, the igloo collapsed; the last bit of snow left on our street was where the igloo had been. But that was in April! Before that we sent off the 30 shillings from the collection box to the Freedom From Hunger Campaign, and thought no more about it until...

In December, whilst I was sitting reading the newspapers in the Students Union Common Room of Swansea University, I started glancing through the Daily Sketch, and saw the main headline on one of the middle pages: "FROM AN IGLOO IN TUNBRIDGE WELLS...." Sure enough, it was about MY Newlands Road Igloo. The paper was listing some of the more unusual ways money had been collected, and there was a short bit about us.

1987 was the next really snowy winter, and the Kent & Sussex Courier repeated the picture of our Newlands Road igloo within a story about the 1963 winter. But although there was a lot of snow in 1987, it did not last as long as 3 or more months, but only

mothers by real sturdy flesh-and-blood example just how important it is that they ensure plenty of proteins, a well-balanced diet, for their young.

And showing the fathers, too, how essential it is that they adopt the new methods they are being taught to drag the last ounce of sustenance from their soil.

Orchard

Boys like Ram, or Bhajan, or Sita are now taking part in a school orchard scheme in many villages. After a short training course, teachers show them how to utilise the last inch of land around the clay classrooms, how to raise bananas, papayas, pineapples, mangoes where only dust rose before.

They put my name on a plaque when I ceremonially planted a fruit-tree in a new orchard near Basti and when I stood up and looked at the eager and lively young faces around me I felt they'd

FROM AN IGLOO IN TUNBRIDGE WELLS...

planted a seed in my heart too.

That is why I want to tell you today how best you can help bring a smile like Ram's to the face of young India.

Many people, for instance, have already promised to follow the Queen Mother's lead and send the cost of an extra place at the Christmas table or an extra name on the gift-list.

Teenagers are planning "Help the Hungry" parties and charging half-a-crown admission. Offices and factories are starting collections.

Little Christine Jeffree, just nine, of Birchwood-road, Maidstone, formed what she calls the "Stop and Go Helping Club" — they sell sweets and gifts to raise money.

Mrs. Cronton, of Presteigne in Radnorshire, who is 74, does a paper-round . . . Peggy and Jenny Smith, of St. Paul's Cray, Kent, gave up sweets during Lent . . . Trinity Academy children in Edinburgh ran a Punch and Judy show . . . angler J. W. Martin of Broadstairs caught a sea-trout and sold it for 30s. . . . pocket money of 5s. 6d. arrived from Carole Wilkes of Bletchley.

Parties

Bristol schoolchildren held sausage parties, juke-box jury sessions, sold toffee apples . . . Cheltenham College boys exhibited their schoolwork to raise £80 of their £1,200 target . . . Glastonbury's mayor, Douglas Osmond, ran a hop-scotch contest.

I admire the imagination of Jane Humphrey and her friends of Tunbridge Wells who built "Britain's biggest igloo" in last winter's cold spell—and charged passers-by to look inside.

Newbury girls Lynette Caesar and Joan Shepherd bet boyfriends they could walk 14 miles to Reading —and won the wager for Freedom From Hunger. Aldermaston girls darned socks for local bachelors.

And so this fine work goes on and on. Esher carol-singers take over Trafalgar-square a week on Saturday. Blundell School boys from Tiverton will sit as the Three Wise Men on the Royal Exchange steps just before Christmas, urging Londoners to contribute.

Isn't there an idea here for you to help the Christmas Babies?

So far, from the people of Britain, £6,000,000 has been raised or promised. Ten times as much, a hundred times, still would not come near solving the problem . . . but every penny really does count, as I saw on my 4,000-mile tour of India.

Health

It takes £450 to put one village on the road to health and vitality. I leave you with this frightening thought:

There are 550,000 villages in desperate need of help.

And suffering in the shade of their mud-hut walls, countless millions of children who could look as happy as little Ram if you will take them to your hearts this Christmas.

When you have raised your gift, here's where to send it:
FREEDOM FROM HUNGER, LONDON, W.C.99.

I admire the imagination of Jane Humphrey and her friends of Tunbridge Wells who built "Britain's biggest igloo" in last winter's cold spell—and charged passers-by to look inside.

about two weeks.

This last photo shows David Stevens sitting on the top with Bronwen, myself and I think Ann Stevens.

David now lives in the house shown!

26) Other Ideas & Events - Street Hall?

I have probably left a few things out, but one little group I have a single picture of. My parents got together with a small group of families, which seemed to be centred upon our next door neighbours at number 17. They were Mr & Mrs John & Joan Hodgson, who were part of the "Trutex" clothing manufacturers of

Kenneth Phillips, Peter Wells, Iluska Wells, Russel Hodgson, Margaret Philips (just behind my Sister) Bronwen, then Betty Jenkins, Joan Hodgson, Julia Hodgson, John Hodgson, Clive Jenkins, and Mr Jenkins. I took the picture.

Clitheroe, Lancashire. I think this picture was taken the day the Hodgsons paid a visit after they had moved away; John was promoted to Manager and they moved up to Clitheroe. In the picture are the Phillips family, The Wells family, & the Jenkins family, as well as the Hodgsons. They called their house in Clitheroe

"Newlands", because they so loved Newlands Road.

Because of all the activity going on in our road, I wrote a page article in "The Newlands Post". As the scan of the original is not too clear I am copying it, but abridged.

ORIGINAL CONTRIBUTIONS.

History Of Newlands Road Area (By Christopher Phillips)

Newlands Road was begun in the middle 1930s, we believe it was to have been a by-pass to Tonbridge, which accounts for its width and its grass verges, and it is now one of the most pleasant roads in Tunbridge Wells. The road is almost free of traffic, except for "L" Drivers and is thus used as an elongated playground.

One of the first organisations was "My Olympic Games" started in 1948, when this became an annual event until 1952. The last sports were held, run by adults, in 1953 at the special Coronation Party. This was held in one of the last remaining fields of Mr Cheesman's farm, in the valley, and was a really big affair.

The second organisation was the annual Newlands Road Firework Display, first put on on Nov 5th 1950, and run, for the first 3 years, by John Burton & Bobby Ely. House To House collections were started and in the first year about £3 was collected. In the following years collections grew & grew until in 1957 £22 was collected, Of this £5 : 5 : 0 Went to Dr Barnardos Homes. In the years 1955 - 7, the show was officially opened by the Mayor of Tunbridge Wells. There was also a torchlight procession and a Guy Competition.

The next organisation was the Scout Fair I organised in our back garden & garage. It was claimed to be "The smallest fair in The World". That ran for 3 years from 1951, and raised about £7 for scout funds.

This society, The Newlands Road Philatelic society,

(This article was in the "Newlands Post", remember, but this article was distributed separately as well*) has, apart from the Firework Display,* (at the time of writing) *been running the longest, and is likely to run for many years to come. It is this club that has broadcast Newlands Road all over SE England* (Radio news) *and advertised it all over the world* (In stamp magazines).

The above activities are of course not the only ones; others begun, some still going, are: "The Newlnads Road Nature Club" (Now the N.R. Science Club) run by Clive Jenkins, Bronwen Phillips & Margaret Collier; "The Kember Friendly Society" (Now the Boys' Club) run by Michael Kember; The N.R. Puppet Club, run by Colin Fowle; and the N.R. Magic Circle, run by myself. These last two have now closed. There is also the "Good companions" run by Phyllchen Herrick and The "Tudor Rose Stamp Club" run by David Reich & Patrick Hoyte (Became part of the N.R.P.S. eventually). I believe that Andrew Knight had also tried his hand at running a small fete.

*Only one event was run by adults: the Coronation party being the exception. (*When I wrote this in the late 1950s I forgot about the end of the WW2 bonfire party in 1945.) *Newlands Road must be one of the most self junior organised roads in the world, as it is the children who get together and run the clubs etc. I suppose it will be the children again who will have to start a Hall for Newlands Road. This is what we need, a small hall for our own entertainments, where parties, dances, concerts, amateur productions, film shows and club meetings can be held. This would cost many hundreds of pounds; surely most families would be able to afford a 2 to 5 pound donation to help put up such a hall with about 300 homes in the area, at £2 per home that would bring in £600. Surely if people can afford*

£20 to burn on fireworks once a year then it can afford £1000 for a permanent hall. We would need to do some of the work ourselves. WOULD THE PEOPLE OF NEWLANDS ROAD AND THE NEARBY ROADS HELP?

Talk it over with your parents & friends. Ideas & offers to 15 Newlands Road, Tunbridge Wells please. (Below this was a map of the streets - Newlands Road, Newlands Rise, Newlands Way, Eastcliff Road, Wilman Road, New England Road and Riddlesdale Avenue.)

In a way, sadly nothing came of this. It was just a dream that never became reality.

So ends this story. A story of a bygone age, before the motor car, TV, computers, and mobile phones took over our lives, a time when people of all ages did things more themselves. There was rationing at the beginning, wages and earnings were generally low, and it cost only 2½ OLD pence to send a letter anywhere in the UK & Ireland. People ate REAL food, and washed and prepared it themselves; eating out, apart from tea, coffee & cakes, was a real treat. People actually went to the cinema every week. No bingo halls, no Ten Pin Bowling. People actually joined drama clubs, played bowls, went dancing, played football and cricket, and had allotments and grew their own food. I am not saying they don't still do those things but it was more the norm back then.

Back then you would never see families or groups eating out in restaurants, texting and talking to their friends on their mobiles at the same time!

I am not saying what happens now is WRONG; it is just different. Without the World Wide Web, I would never have gone on a 4 month journey round the world to meet people, whom I had only "met" online, in

8 countries, and been taken to out-of-the-way places, and met people of different races and cultures. One of those I met on this journey was Chris Yardley, who apparently bought our NRPS FDCs, but I could not trace his personal membership. His brother (Michael) and sister (Elizabeth) had joined and Elizabeth had been one of the elected Officers in the later years, and his father had once been one of the judges. Chris now lives in Canberra, Australia. This was the subject of my previous book "**Around The World In 128 Days Minus 1**", which is available on Amazon Kindle. (Over 300 pages, 80 in full colour). I am expecting to have this book on Kindle as well.

Since then I have met (at the time of writing) 68 Internet friends in person, from 14 countries (Canada, USA, Argentina, New Zealand, Australia, The Philippines, Hong Kong, Singapore, Malta, Romania, Israel, Palestine, Thailand and Croatia). Many internet friends have also come to stay a few days with us.

And I would never be publishing my own books, if it were not for computers and the World Wide Web. Yes I was an English "O" Level failure, twice!

So some changes have been GOOD.

The Igloo after a slight thaw

27) Appendices

Index of people, clubs & publications
(Just a number means their **NRPS** membership number)
Key to clubs :- **N** = Newlands Rd Club; **P** = Puppet ; **M** = Magic Circle; **B** = Bottle Top & Bible Reading; **NC** = Nature Club; **F** = Fireworks displays. **G** = Good Companions; **T** = Tudor Rose S C; **K** = Kember Friendly Society

Children living in Wilman Road; Eastcliff Road; Riddlesdale Avenue; New England Road

Peter Veness	31	108; 132
Patrick Hoyte	18	57; 61; 80; 83; 85; 86; 87; 88; 89; 94; 108; 110; 111; 149; 159; 181
Humphrey Smeeton	F	33; 54; 79
Penelope Hoyte	36	
Margaret Collier	49	73; 83; 84; 91; 111; 181
Caroline Collier	65	88; 91
Brian Campsie	9	21; 25; 54
Raymond Perryman	29	
Michael Kember	? ; K	181
Phyllchen Herrick	51; G	108; 181
Rowland Holland	82	
Charlotte Herrick	35; G	
Hugh Maitland	46	

Children living elsewhere in Tunbridge Wells or nearby

David Reich	19	61; 80; 85; 87; 88; 108; 159; 181
David Beeby	20	65; 83; 111
Lynda Bringloe	80	89; 155; 157; 158; 159; 164; 168
Shirley Burr	78	63; 84; 87; 89; 91; 111; 155; 158; 159; 168
Erica Schoolar	93	
David Green	101	63; 72; 84; 87; 89; 155; 159; 165; 168
Simon Levitt	40	61; 83; 85; 86
Christopher Selmes	21	61; 83; 85; 86; 87; 91; 128
Ian Myers		25
Susan Smith TW	67	62; 83; to 87; 111; 112; 124; 156; 159; 168
John Botten	22	
Christina Hindle	60	108
Patrick Smith	68	62; 83; 84; 86; 88; 111; 112
Robert Romer	94	89; 159; 165; 166
Peter Lewis	?	61; 80
Christopher Bayly	?	80; 87
Mark Nicholson	108	84; 87; 160
Andrew Crighton	?	164; 165

name	Club

Not mentioned in this book, but were members of the NRPS living elsewhere in Tunbridge Wells or near by

Dudley Waters	31
David Truckle	18
Jeffrey ?	F
John Botten	36
Lance Terry	49
Neil Coxhead	65
Peter Crayford	9
Andrew Kingham	29
David Rose	? ; K
Francis Hodgkinson	51; G
Michael Samuels	29
William Mayling	82
John Fry	35; G
Barry Coleman	52
Keith Parker	53
David Digby	54
Andrew Hopkins	55
Michael Powell	56
Geraldine Lea	57
Richard Beckwith	58
Michael Wellman	59
Michael Beckwith	??

Name	page

NRPS Members living in other parts of UK & the world

Margaret Price (Grimsby)	38 P
Paul Marotte (Paris France)	44P
David Keating (Edgeware	57P 89
Noel Harrington (Cork, Eire)	61P
Robert Corag	74P
Hamish Kirk	76P

Adults Living in Newlands Road, Rise or Way

John Hodgson	51; 53; 79; 179
Betty Jenkins	57; 80; 179
Mr Muffet	34; 61; 180
Mrs Muffet	57; 61; 80
Norman Timmis	94
Mr Cheeseman	9; 15; 38; 51
Kenneth Phillips	16; 45; 51; 176;l 179
Margaret Phillips	13; 17; 45; 179
The Collier Family	?
Anna Newton	13
Mr Jenkins	179
Mr Burton	?
Mr Yardley	80

Appendices

Index of people, clubs & publications

15 Newlands Road now (2016) The pear tree is still there!

Games & Activities

Roads, Towns & Places etc

28) Formal documents from the council re Newlands Road

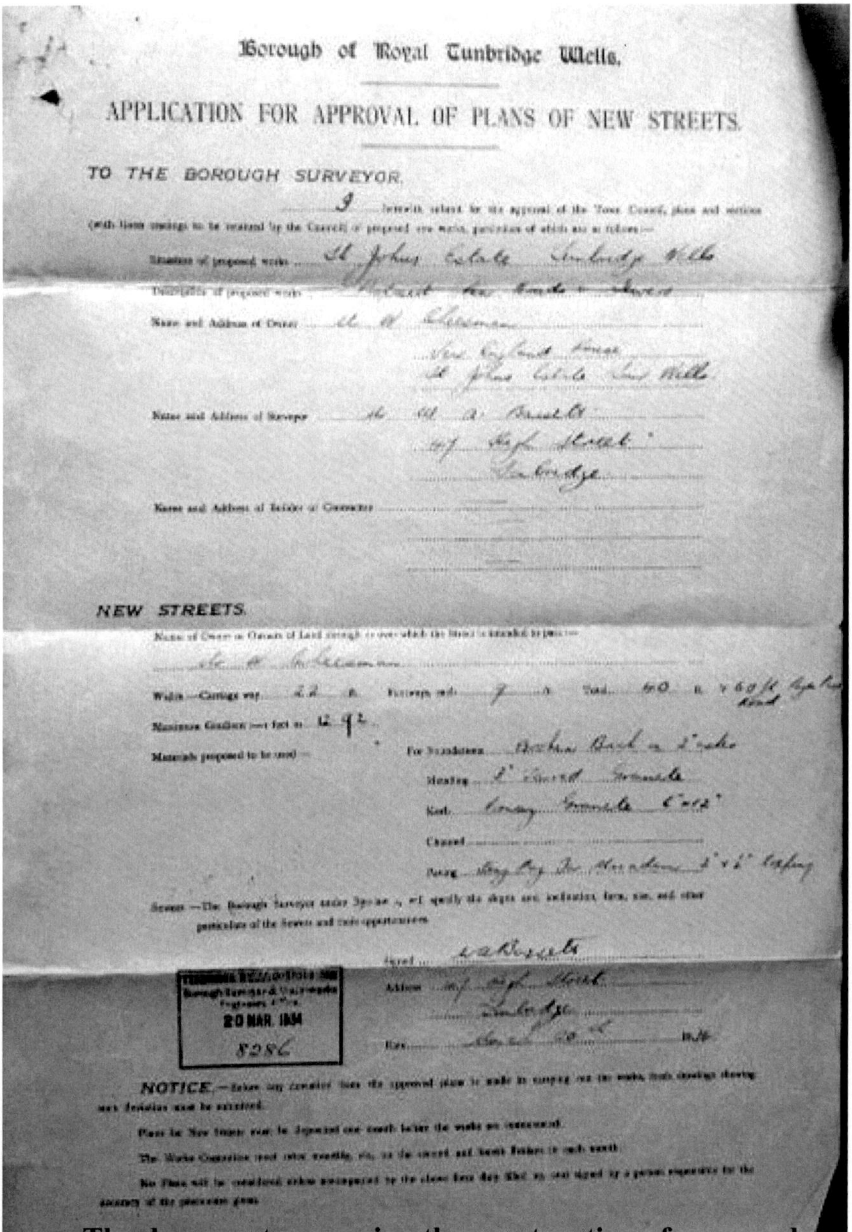

Borough of Royal Tunbridge Wells.

APPLICATION FOR APPROVAL OF PLANS OF NEW STREETS.

TO THE BOROUGH SURVEYOR.

NEW STREETS.

TUNBRIDGE WELLS BOROUGH
Borough Surveyor & Waterworks
Engineer's Office
20 MAR. 1934
8286

NOTICE.

The document approving the construction of new roads on the Newlands Farm Estate. 20 Mar 1934

Central Chambers,
47, High Street,
TONBRIDGE.

March 26th, 1934.

To,
H.P. Bishop, Esq., M.I.M.C.E.,
Borough Engineer & Surveyor,
1 & 2, Calverley Mount,
Tunbridge Wells.

Dear Sir,

Re: St. John's Estate, Tunbridge Wells.

Referring to your Committee's Disapproval of the plans submitted by me for new roads and sewers on the above Estate, I understand that the reason for disapproval was that the footpaths were shewn to be finished in Tar Macadam and not in brick paving as is now your specification.

I would however point out that when the first set of plans were submitted for this estate the whole of the development was shewn and the portion not being proceeded with at the time was marked "Future Development". The finish of the footpaths on these plans was tar macadam as was also the finish shewn on the plan recently approved for the extension of Wilman Road, under these circumstances it seems very extraordinary to disapprove of the finish of the footpaths for the next portion of the development when the whole development has already been approved and is being carried out in sections.

In view of the above facts I shall be much obliged if you will recommend your Committee to approve the plans and agree to the same finish as Wilman Road which has just been made up to your requirements.

Regarding the names for the new roads it has been decided to call the Bye Pass Road "Newlands Road" and the road connecting with the extension of Wilman Road "Newlands Rise", which names I trust will meet with approval.

I shall be glad to hear from you at earliest I am anxious to get the work started.

Yours faithfully,

(Sgd). W.A. BASSETT.

An extraordinary letter, naming the link roads as the Rise & Way, and the pavement surfaces.

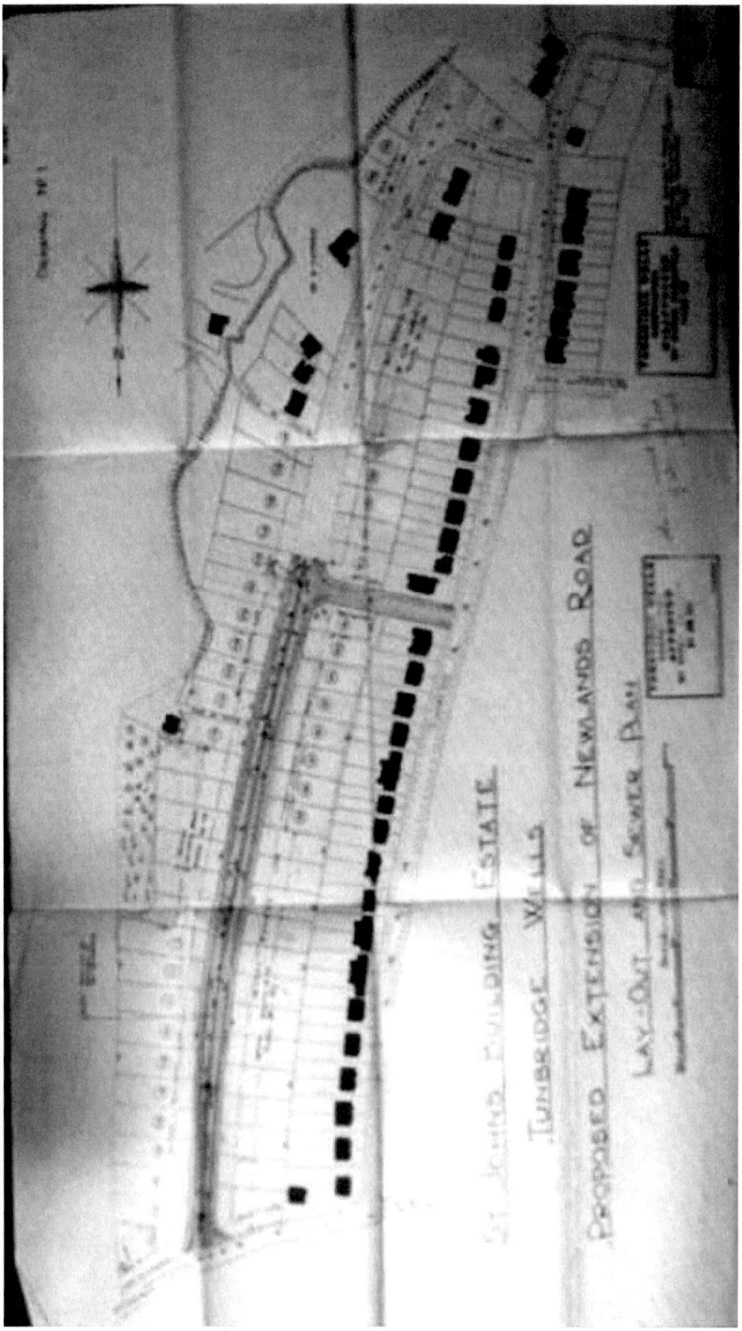

Plans for the upper part of Newlands Road

Plan showing position of Newlands Road, and other roads in Red; the other 2 were never completed. The date of this is unknown, but was before Wilman Road and Eastcliff Road had been extended beyond Mereworth Road. It shows where they had intended Newlands Road to have joined Somerset Road.

The architect's plans for our house (Also the house next door)

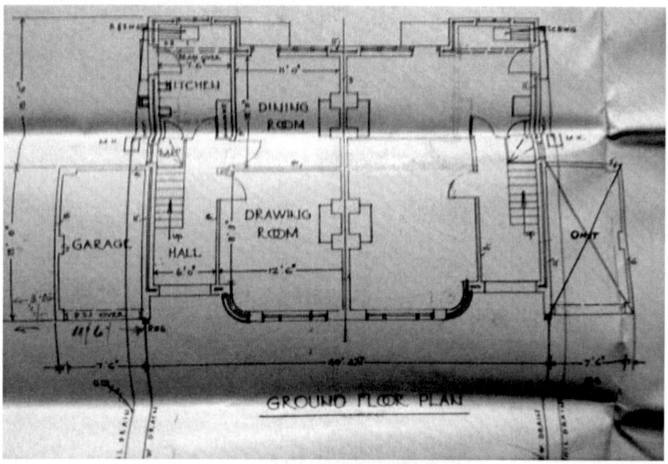

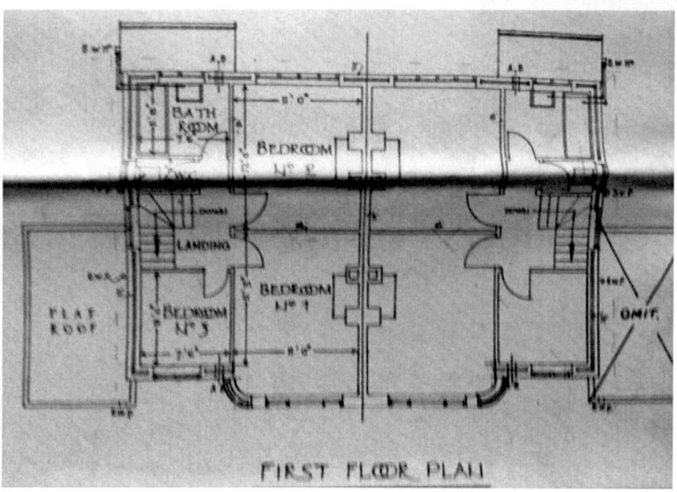

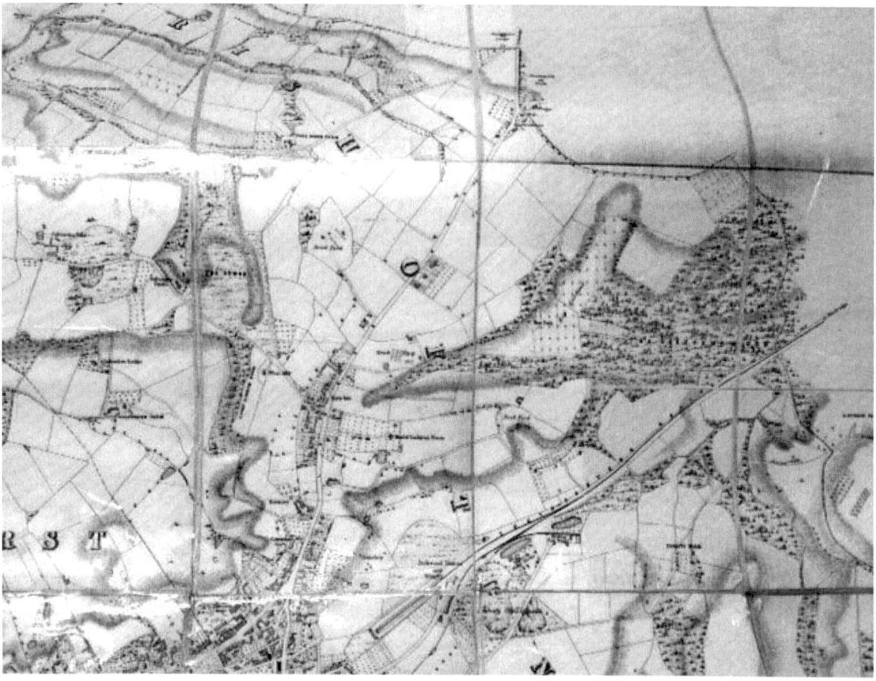
R S T

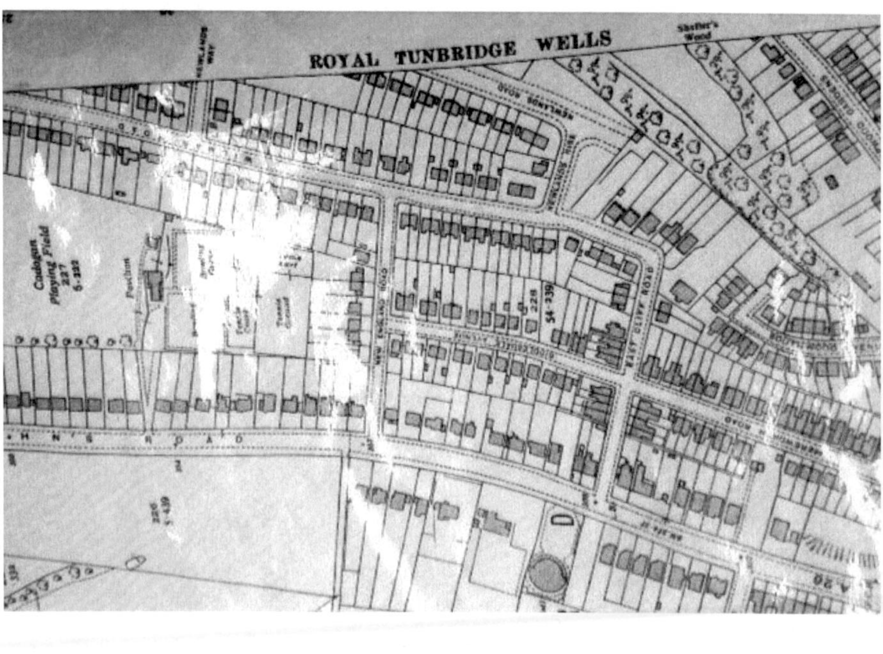
ROYAL TUNBRIDGE WELLS
Cadogan Playing Field
Pavilion

The approval for my Dad to have the garage built in the back garden, in 1949.

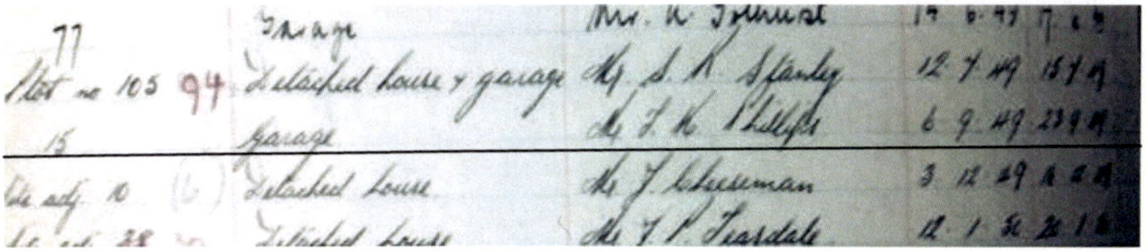

77	Garage	Mr. [illegible]	14.6.49	[illegible]
Plot no 105 94	Detached house & garage	Mr S. K. Stanley	12.7.49	15.7.49
15	Garage	Mr T. K. Phillips	6.9.49	23.9.49
[illegible] 10 (6)	Detached house	Mr J. [illegible]	3.12.49	[illegible]

Year 2016 Photos of Newlands Road

Newlands Rise, where we had the sledging in the snowy winters

Newlands Road from bottom of Newlands Rise, looking north.

Newlands Road; where the two houses on the right were not built in 1951, we had the first few Bonfires & firework displays

Newlands Road, where the Bonfire party moved to almost opposite, till these 3 houses were built in the mid 1950s, then we only had the Firework displays

Book already published,

available direct from the author or on Amazon Kindle

"Around the World in 128 Days Minus 1"

ISBN 978-0-9574259-0-3

(About my meeting over 30 of my internet friends on a 4 month journey to 8 countries)

Review By Carrie Bagnell Horsburgh

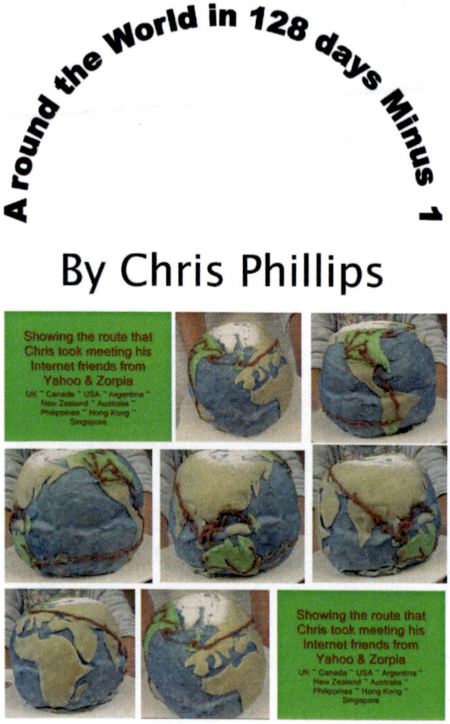

What a great little book! I know the author and was lucky enough to be one of the people he visited on his around the world trip. (I'm in the book!) Chris is not an author by trade, so I found this read more like letters or diary entries from a friend. Not to say it wasn't full of adventure!

He got to meet some really neat people and visit incredibly interesting places around the world. And there are lots of pictures included that Chris took during his trip. I learned a lot from reading this book. A bit of history, religion, geography, botany, and of animals I had never heard of. There are also other little interesting tid-bits of information that were peppered throughout. This book would also be a useful resource for anyone planning a trip to one of the places Chris visited. He's included names of hotels he stayed at, vegetarian restaurants he visited and websites, addresses and phone numbers of other places of interest. What an exciting experience and I'm so glad he decided to share it with us. But watch for quokka to pop up on the Scrabble board Chris! :)

Another review on next page